Born a Jew... Die a JEW

THE STORY OF MARTIN CHERNOFF
A PIONEER IN MESSIANIC JUDAISM

Messianic Ministries, Inc.

BY
YOHANNA CHERNOFF

WITH JIMI MILLER

Born a JEW ...Die a JEW

Copyright © 1996 by Yohanna Chernoff

All rights reserved.

All Scripture quotations are from the New Berkeley Version of the Bible, © 1945, 1959, 1969 by Hendrickson Publishers, Inc., unless otherwise noted. References marked NKJ are from the New King James Version of the Bible © copyright 1979, 1980, 1982 by Thomas Nelson, Inc., Nashville, Tennessee. References Marked KJV are from the Authorized King James Version of the Bible. References marked TLB are from The Living Bible, copyright © 1971 by Tyndale House Publishers, Inc., Wheaton, Illinois.

Published by:

Messianic Ministries, Inc.
P.O. Box 1024
Havertown, PA 19083

ISBN 9781980931843

Printed in the United States of America
For Worldwide Distribution

Write the vision! Make it plain ... that he who runs by may read it! However, the vision waits for its appointed time; it hastens toward the end; it will not lie. If it lingers, wait for it; for it will certainly come; it will not lag. ... But the righteous shall live by his faith.
Habakkuk 2:2-4

Contents

Preface vii

Part I:..1
1. Breaking Chains (1880-1908)..................................3
2. The Long Journey (1908-1928) 9
3. Running From God (1928-1940) 21
4. A Stranger In A Strange Land (1940-1949) 29
5. My Own Search (1930-1946) 39
6. A Twentieth-Century Ruth (1946-1949) 47
7. Two Become One (1949-1953).............................57

Part II:...71
8. Clashes With the Establishment Church (1953-1960)..73
9. The Second Vision (1961-1966) 89
10. Winds of Change (1965-1967) 97
11. A New Thing Coming (1967).............................109
12. A Crossroads (1968-1969) 113
13. The Third Vision - Messianic Judaism (1970)..123
14. The Prayer Meeting (1970-1971).......................133
15. The Joy of Messianic Judaism (1972) 143
16. *Yeshua* - the Great Physician (1972-1973) 153
17. The New Wine (1973-1975) 159

PART III 181
18. Opposition (1975-1979).......................................183
19. *Sukkot* - The Great Festival of Messianic Judaism (1980-1984) 199
20. If We Can Destroy *Beth Yeshua* ... (1984-1985) .211
21. Rabbi Martin, Rabbi David (1985).....................227
22. New Wine to Come (Post 1985).........................235
23. A Prophecy By Rabbi Martin Chernoff 245

Bibliography..249

PREFACE

I have fought the good fight...   2 Timothy 4:7

Pioneering in Messianic Judaism has never been easy. Three stunning visions were given from the Almighty God to my late husband, Martin M. Chernoff, beginning in the fall of 1948. In progressive steps, each vision unveiled its own aspect of a wondrous phenomenon developing on the horizon - a mighty spiritual revival of Jewish souls into the Kingdom of God. During Marty's remaining thirty-seven tumultuous years, his submission to that single, unfolding vision, revealed in three stages, never wavered.

The vision itself never relinquished its iron hold on his heart. Once he saw it, he held it clear in his mind. We always somehow knew, but did not always see, that spiritually we were swimming upstream over waterfalls, around boulders and dams, against undercurrents and the tides of man's traditions, which the Word of God decries: *"You have nullified the Word of God through your tradition"* (Matthew 15:6). Even as we saw that God was creating something new, for a long time we did not recognize it as a worldwide movement away from traditions and into God's revival truth.

Marty was born in 1920 in Toronto, Canada, the fifth of six children, to Russian Jewish immigrant parents. Both shy and independent, Marty became confused in his youth by the conflicting priorities of a strictly kosher home life and the basically Christian, Canadian public-school system and longed to live his own life in his own way.

God, however, had a different plan for him. In 1941, Marty accepted *Yeshua* (Hebrew for Jesus) as his Messiah and Savior, gaining absolute assurance of his personal salvation after reading Charles Finney's *Revival Lectures* for the first time. Marty gained confidence that he, like Finney, was also called to "pray down a revival," and his life soon became eternally focused upon service to the Lord as both *M'vaser* (evangelist) and visionary.

I first met this amazing man in 1949, on campus at the University of Tennessee. I was a sophomore, and he had come to speak to the Jewish students about prophecy in *the Tanah* (Old Covenant or Testament). The Lord had already infused my heart with a deep, supernatural love for the Jewish people, a love that has never let me go. Consequently, during Marty's one week on campus, I developed a great appreciation for him. He was such a knowledgeable, spiritual, God-fearing Jewish believer in the Messiah of Israel that later that same year I married him.

In early 1967, Marty experienced for himself the mighty pouring out of God's Holy Spirit on all flesh promised by the prophets of old (Joel 2:28, Acts 2:17), and sensed the first stirring among others of an imminent Jewish restoration to belief in *Yeshua* of Nazareth, as Israel's long-expected Messiah. He longed to see the removal of what the Messianic Jewish Shaliah Shaul (Apostle Paul) referred to as Israel's *"partial insensibility [blindness]"* so that *"Israel will be saved"* (Romans 11:25-26).

Basically a very humble man, Marty accomplished much of what God called him to do either on his knees, or pacing back and forth, crying out directly into the ear of the Almighty. After long periods of extended prayer and fasting, Marty, in the course of time, would emerge from these seasons of prayer with a renewed direction in our calling. Although God thrust Marty into the limelight of the Messianic Jewish Movement, usually against his will (much like Moses and other spiritual leaders in the Scriptures), he always won his victories in his daily prayer closet with the Lord.

In 1967 Marty felt strongly that Israel's astonishing June victory in the Arab-Israeli Six Day War was a major prophetic milestone, and he pondered his own role in God's unfolding plan.

In early partial fulfillment of the vision, God used Marty mainly as visionary-revivalist, and He used me mainly as visionary-pragmatist, and each of our three children as pioneers to blaze trails and plant the seeds, in America and overseas, of what is recognized today as Messianic Judaism. Since then, in the face of both subtle and flagrant opposition, we openly and purposefully began turning many believers in *Yeshua* the Messiah back to their Jewish roots.

While we watched the impact diffusing abroad, we discerned two parallel phenomena: "Political Zionism," finding its expression in the establishment of the nation of Israel, advocating the return of the Jewish people to their Land; and a new "Spiritual Zionism," finding its expression in Messianic Judaism, advocating the acceptance of *Yeshua* as the Jewish Messiah by Jewish people, while, at the same time, remaining Jews in lifestyle and identity.

Marty set us all an example. Steadfastly he blazed a trail and laid a foundation, so that those who followed could see what can be accomplished through prayer and obedience, and could perhaps do *"greater things than these"* in *Yeshua's* name. With his left hand, he birthed the congregation; with his right hand, he nurtured the international Messianic Movement, participating in all the battles. Thrust into the limelight, he became recognized as a revivalist with a vision, and almost as renown as a mighty prayer warrior.

I believe that there are many Messianic rabbis who are revivalists today because we dared to plant the first seeds. Unquestionably, there were other Messianic believers who were moved upon by God in somewhat the same way at the same time. But with no one to ask, we had to formulate the radical ideas and concepts pretty much on our own. Consequently, we caught a lot of the first bullets.

To introduce you to Messianic Judaism's American roots, through our work as pioneers in the movement, is my purpose in writing this book. I herein share with you our trials and testings, and the incomparable joy inherent in the birthing of a "new thing" into the Body of believers, that has every indication of growing into a Movement that will impact the world, lead many Jews and Gentiles into the Kingdom of God, and help prepare the way for the soon return of the Messiah *Yeshua.*

The Lord blessed both my husband and me with countless timely and pertinent verses of Scripture, as He led us on our journey in pursuit of the Messianic vision. Along the way, I studied many translations of the Bible, combining them, working them together, often comparing them with the original Hebrew, Greek or Aramaic, accepting the most relevant meaning in each situation as I saw it. Along with the retelling of our story herein, I share these with you.

My story, as Mrs. Martin Chernoff, reflects God's call, not only on the remarkable man I married, but also on myself and on each of our three children: Joel, our royal musician; David, our son, the rabbi; and Hope, our youth worker and women's leader, our shining candle.

I believe the best way for me to introduce Marty is by reviewing his parents' history and a little of their background as Russian Jewish emigrants from the infamous White Russian Pale of Settlement, to America.

As you walk with us through these pages - my humble attempt to reveal who we are, what we are, and how we got here - may God bless and encourage you to follow your own call, as we did ours, with commitment, perseverance and joy, keeping your eye always on the goal He sets before you.

May He also draw you into a deeper understanding of what He is so gloriously accomplishing today among His beloved Jewish people throughout our world.

And so my story begins...

Yohanna Chernoff
Philadelphia
June 1996

PART I

Chapter One

Breaking Chains

...famine is there, and if we remain here we shall die. Now come, let us desert ... if they spare us, we shall live; if they kill us, we shall just die.
                                                                2 Kings 7:4

1880-1908: Flight from the Pale

In Eastern Europe, in the late nineteenth century, the White Russian Pale of Settlement, an enormous land area known simply as the Pale, encompassed the entire realm of Jewish communities in southern and western Russia, the Ukraine, Lithuania, Byelorussia, and much of eastern Poland - 386,000 square miles stretching from the Baltic to the Black Sea.

The year before Russia's infamous 1881 Massacre of the Jews, Solomon Chernoff, who would one day become Marty's father, was born within the borders of the Pale in the decrepit little *shtetl* (shantytown) of Chechersk, where shocking poverty, frustrated striving, and haunting loneliness hung over its inhabitants.

On January 19, the year following the Massacre, about ten miles down the rickety railroad tracks from Chechersk, Marty's mother Yelena was born to the Shandling family in the *shtetl* of Propoisk, a jumble of wooden houses clustering about the market place, where to own a wooden floor was a sign of extreme affluence.

The squalid villages of Propoisk and Chechersk were

typical of the impoverished strongholds of Jewish life in Eastern Europe, with their many poor shopkeepers, peddlers, pawnbrokers, artisans, innkeepers and distillers. Their very existence was, at best, tenuous, tied, as it eternally was, to the wretched economy of the Russian peasantry and the whim of the reigning Czar. Harsh natural and social conditions, combined with poor soil, made the lot of the Jews of the White Russian Pale the most miserable of all Eastern Europeans.

Solomon, the youngest of ten children, eight of them boys, shared with his siblings a fierce determination to escape the terrible life of the Jew in the Russian Pale. His oldest brother left Russia before 1900, settled in New York City, and, almost immediately, prospered well enough tailoring, "hustling the needles trade," as it was then called, to begin sending money home for his other brothers to follow him to North America. And follow they did, one after another, each settling in a different city - Chicago, Montreal, Rochester, Buffalo, Pittsburgh and Philadelphia - and, sadly, eventually losing touch with one another altogether.

Yelena Shandling and her sister Khasia, both blue-eyed, strawberry-blondes, were possibly the prettiest girls in their village. Full of fun and laughter, in spite of the barrenness surrounding them, they loved to swim in the nearby Dnieper River, whenever they could slip away.

Like Solomon, Yelena-the-dreamer also dreamed of high adventure in America. Every time a letter from someone's relatives in that faraway land arrived in the village, she dreamed of sailing away with her future husband - whoever he might be - on the next boat, to a new life in the New World, where she would walk on streets of gold.

It was a time of dreams and a time of nightmares for

Breaking Chains

the Jews, as even *shtetl* life disintegrated under the double hammer of the evil, anti-Semitic Czar Alexander II's elitist, economic oppression, and the Pale' s own inner spiritual decay.

Still, within the abject poverty and privation of life in the Pale, Solomon and Yelena met and married, and had a son, Israel.

But Solomon was soon conscripted to serve his compulsory term in the Russian Army, where the Jewish soldiers were actually prodded by their officers to sacrifice their lives to the glory of the Czar. Oftentimes, Jewish soldiers were intentionally pushed to the front lines to handle the initial wave of fighting, because- they were "expendable."

After several years, Solomon realized that if he stayed in the Czar's army much longer he just might accommodate the Czar's wishes. Upon hearing more and more rumors and reports of jobs and fortunes to be made in America, he squirreled away all the money he could obtain from both families along with all the money his older brother sent from New York, and made his plans to desert the Army, and then flee to America with his wife and son.

To the uneducated Russian Jews, any place on either the North or South American continent was considered "America." The fare for one passage to the east coast of America was $25 total, or so they were told.

Desperate to escape, in 1905, Solomon, Yelena and little Israel, with their small cache of coins and a set of forged papers rolled in oilcloth, set out during a treacherous snow storm on their illegal, dangerous, and extortionate journey. They would travel by train from Propoisk to the port city of Odessa, Russia, where they would board a ship for Amsterdam, Holland. There was no way for them to travel quickly and safely, and sometimes they had to walk.

By the time they reached Holland months had passed, and their funds were depleted. As a result of the endless bribes and forced payoffs along the way (their forged papers fooled no one), they finally found themselves on the streets of Amsterdam, a strange city in a strange country, without money, without friends, without a place to sleep. They were hungry and cold. Yelena and little Israel were both sick. Their money was gone, their resources exhausted. Like thousands of other Jews before and since, they were stranded.

But they had gotten out. That was the important thing. To have escaped from the sufferings of the Russian Pale meant life and they clung to that hope.

In 1905, to be stranded in Amsterdam, or in Liverpool, or inany other port city along the way, was not unusual for the Jewish immigrant, who, between 1880 and 1914, was the object of international big business.

Ruthless agents of large European steamship lines contrived get-rich-quick schemes at the cruel expense of the three million Jews making mass exodus from Russia to America. As a result, many Jews were intentionally detained until the agents could route them to wherever they themselves could realize the highest profits. Argentina, for example, actively sought Russian Jewish immigrants to help expand and colonize her vast territory.

Labor-hungry markets in the fast-growing, industrialized cities of North America had also joined hands with the large steamship lines, each having its own recruiters in every country. A callous bounty system developed that often defrauded the naive immigrant of his hard-earned, already insufficient funds.

Exorbitant steerage and food costs aboard ship, as well as the alarming specter of seasickness, while dreaded,

Breaking Chains

were at least anticipated. But, the real pitfalls - the unexpected and escalating costs - came from having to deal with governments, agents and hustlers. The $25 advertised price of passage to the New World, for example, was nothing more than a spurious statistic. One could be bilked of more money on the journey from home to port, or even while detained at the harbor, than the eventual cost of the actual voyage. Boarding ship and ultimately landing in the New World were both fraught with danger and heartache.

How Solomon, Yelena and little Israel managed to survive for three years in Amsterdam, while waiting to accumulate the fare and finding the right ship, is anyone's guess. Perhaps one of the Jewish relief societies springing up in the port cities helped them. Perhaps someone in the family sent more money. Perhaps Solomon simply learned to hustle, to survive on the streets of the little free country of Holland as one of the *Luftmensch* ("airman," a person with no visible means of support), or, like his older brother, by hustling the needles trade. No one knows.

Finally, in November 1908, the long-awaited day came. They boarded ship and set sail for New York City - or so they believed. Unknown to them, the ship they were on was actually headed to South America. Eventually, they disembarked. They had gone as far as their meagre fares would take them and they stepped off the ship. They were in Buenos Aires, Argentina.

Chapter Two

The Long Journey

I will counsel you with My eye. Psalm 32:8

1908-1928: Buenos Aires, Toronto

To Solomon and Yelena, Buenos Aires in December was lush, semitropical, mostly uninhabited jungle - quite different from their familiar, frigid Russian winter. Anti-Semitism was practically nonexistent. But even as Solomon conscientiously plied his "needles trade" (tailoring), the highly lauded plentiful jobs and easy money were not forthcoming for him. For the expecting fair-skinned, fair-haired Yelena, the sun was too hot, the housing inadequate and disappointing. And so, once again, they began hoarding their money for passage to America, this time straight to New York City, to join Solomon's oldest brother, who wrote them enthusiastic letters about life in New York.

After three years and two more babies (Rose and Sophie), in August 1911, when Solomon was thirty-four years old, and Yelena thirty-two, they boarded ship and left Argentina. After docking somewhere on the southeastern coast of the United States, they continued on by train. Having been informed that the "last stop" in America was New York City, Solomon asked the porter as best he could in his scrambled Yiddish-Spanish-English, to put them off at the "last stop."

Each time the train slowed down, anxious Solomon

would ask the porter, "Is this the last stop?" And the porter would reassure him, "Nope, not the last stop yet."

On September 4, exhausted and once again depleted of funds, with young Israel, Rose and Sophie in tow, Solomon and Yelena finally detrained at the "last stop," which this time turned out to be not New York City, but Toronto, Canada.

Solomon quickly learned that the largest number of immigrants in Toronto came from the Russian Pale. About four thousand had flooded in from Russia, with high hopes and driving ambition to take advantage of the free country, with the free economy and the free educational system. Many had already realized surprisingly successful lives.

From Toronto's train depot, the family was led to St. John's Ward, the immigrant-holding area in the north-central part of the burgeoning metropolis, and Solomon was able to go immediately to work at his needles trade. And so they stayed in Toronto, not realizing that the hand of God had led them to this place at the train's literal "last stop."

Toronto's growth as a city coincided with this large influx of immigrants. Hard-working, ambitious, and confident of improvement, they provided the reservoir of manpower needed by the expanding city.

In St. John's Ward, the Jewish people, Toronto's largest group of immigrants, lived side-by-side with Ukrainians, Moravians, Poles, Finns, Italians, and Chinese. The Ward, which extended north up York Street from the railway station, had first appeared in 1890 as a shantytown, where newcomers crammed into one- and two-story homes. It became the backyard of the main commercial area along Yonge and Queen Streets, near other immigrant housing, with work opportunities for tradesmen and store owners. Crowded mostly with

The Long Journey

small warehouses, factories, and commercial establishments, it was interspersed with smaller boarding houses, shops and foreign storefronts. Christian churches, evangelical missions and social clubs were gathering places for both street preachers and social workers, who served free coffee, soup and friendship.

The Jewish immigrants in Toronto had no way of knowing that, since the early 1900s, God was stirring up, within the mainstream of Christianity, a spiritual renaissance among Jewish believers in *Yeshua*, who at this time were calling themselves "Hebrew Christians." Long before 1896 and the publication of the Zionist leader Herzl's pamphlet, *Der Judenstadt* (The Jewish State), the Spirit of God had been prompting Jews to return to the Land, to *Eretz Israel.* Now, the same Holy Spirit was revitalizing Jewish believers with a renewed desire, not only to reestablish their own identity as Jews, but also to seek the salvation of their own people.

The year 1915 had seen the formation of the Hebrew Christian Alliance of America (HCAA), whose basic purpose was to bring together Jewish believers for fellowship and to be a light to their people. Since then, Jewish people in visible numbers, in the major cities of the United States and England, were coming to a saving knowledge of *Yeshua* as Messiah and Savior and joining the mainstream churches. Among these cities was Toronto, where in the middle of the Ward, at the Hebrew-Christian Congregation, many Jewish people were being born again, speaking out, and standing up to be counted because of the ministry of Sabbati Rohold, a believing Jew born in Palestine from a long line of rabbis, and many others like him.

While remaining virtually unaware of what was happening around them in the spiritual realm, Italian and Jewish traders and street vendors throughout the lanes and unpaved streets of the Ward, peddled their wares: new clothes, secondhand clothes, fruits, vegetables, and housewares. With hardly any distinction between home and shop, backyards were often cluttered with sheds and goods. A cacophony of loud talking, laughing, crying, gossiping, arguing, yelling, singing and banging pots and pans, was their daily fare. But the most important aspect of their lives was news about family, news from home, news from the Old Country.

St. John's Ward was not the only bustling center of Jewish life. The Kensington Market district which, in 1901, had been 80 percent Anglo-Canadian, by 1911 was 100 percent Jewish. Living quarters there were mostly ramshackle and inadequate, until the struggling but determined new residents became home owners and improved them.

Large-scale Jewish settlements, and their expanding commercial establishments, were also spreading out to the west of Kensington Market throughout the garment districts around Spadina Avenue, and the Italians began moving in and settling along College and Dundas Streets. But the Ward and Kensington Market were the main centers of Jewish commerce and socializing, and the streets became the children's noisy playgrounds.

The Jewish women shopped daily for their food. Men lingered over glasses of tea. Families and friends sat on their front stoops in the heat of a summer's day, with children playing everywhere. The women of the Ward and Market colored the atmosphere with their overt friendliness; and, after sunset on Friday nights, Roman-Catholic Italian mothers often scolded their sons for being late to light the *Shabbat* candles for their Orthodox Jewish neighbors, whose religious tradition forbade them to work on their Sabbath day any later than eighteen minutes before sundown.

The Long Journey

With many young men away serving the country in World. War I, Solomon had plenty of work as a tailor; but still the family had to scrape to make ends meet. Often; he did not know if he could provide clothes and shoes for each member of his family. He feared that his own children would have the same foot deformities he still suffered from having worn secondhand, ill-fitting shoes as a child.

In spite of their perpetual relative poverty, Yelena maintained a strict kosher kitchen and oversaw a very strict religious life for her growing brood.

Solomon, or "Sol," as he was then called, was also very religious, attending synagogue every Sabbath, and, for awhile, going each morning to prayer. Gradually, however, the reasons for doing these things dimmed for him in the melting pot of the Anglo-Canadian, Jewish-immigrant culture. But in 1917 something happened to Solomon, a spiritual experience that would change his life, but one that he kept secret from his entire family.

Lonely and in desperate need of encouragement and help, Sol shuffled through the snow on Toronto's Elizabeth Street, dreading to go home to his needy family. Eventually, he came as far as the Hebrew-Christian Congregation, which advertised English classes for all immigrants and a school for men. With acute misgivings, Sol went inside. Once inside, the shelter, the friendliness, the atmosphere of togetherness, the palpable love of God, gave him a strangely warm feeling.

He sat quietly through the class already in session, listening to Rev. Rohold, president of the two-year-old Hebrew Christian Alliance of America, preaching in Yiddish and claim, incredibly, from the Scriptures that *Yeshua* or Jesus of Nazareth was the Messiah.

Sol was stunned. He knew the *Tanah* plainly prophesied a Messiah for the Jews, but how could this be? How could Rev. Rohold's Jesus, the same hated "Christ of the pogroms," of "Death to the Jews!" be the Messiah?

"A true Jewish faith," Rev. Rohold declared boldly, "was fulfilled in *Yeshua* of Nazareth, the Jewish Messiah!" Then the fiery evangelist confronted young Sol Chernoff with a choice which would never have been offered him in the stifling confines of the Pale:

If you confess with your lips the Lord [Yeshua], and believe in your heart that God raised him from the dead, you will be saved. Romans 10:9-10

Sol suddenly gained supernatural understanding that the "Jesus" of the Gentiles' Holy Bible was not - could not be - the same as the "Christ" of the pogroms. Gradually, he came to realize that *Yeshua* of Nazareth actually fulfilled all the biblical prophecies concerning the Messiah, and soon accepted Him as his own Messiah, even praying secretly in His name.

He didn't tell his wife what he had done. Yelena would never understand. Fiercely loyal to the Orthodox Judaism of her childhood, Yelena delighted in the Sabbath, in the lighting of the candles, the blessing of the bread and the wine. She reveled in the prayers in the synagogue services. Whatever her other burdens, she clung to God as her comfort. Until the day she died, she never ate outside her home, trusting in the purity of no kitchen but her own. As for her children, just as fiercely as she saved towards their college educations, she saved for her sons' *bar mitzvahs* and their after-school *heder* (Hebrew school). Yelena remained *frum* (piously orthodox), speaking and reading Yiddish almost exclusively, koshering her meats, making *latkas* (pancakes) and *knaydls* (dumplings) for her family.

The Long Journey

No, Sol could not share his new-found faith with Yelena or with the others. He knew that for him to acknowledge *Yeshua* publicly as the Messiah would drastically change the climate and direction of his life. How could he publicly identify with Christians, who, most Jews believed, had for almost two thousand years relentlessly persecuted his people? He could not. He had friends. He had a business. He had a family, none of whom would ever accept such a radical departure on his part. fie was a hard worker, and the scent of success was very real, the specter of the Pale still too close to ignore. With urgent matters of survival vying for his attention, he could not stop now to get his spiritual house in order. Besides, his life-style of freedom was important to him. Money was his goal. The world was racing by, and he was determined to claim his place on the merry-go-round of life and catch the brass ring of success. He could not get away from the fact that he believed, but he would have to hide that belief away in his heart for a future time.

Sol worked hard and soon he was able to move his family into their first real home, 38 Kensington Avenue, near the Fish Market. Somehow they were able to buy the house before their fourth child, Yaacov (Jacob), was born in 1918.

Meanwhile, years after the so-called European Enlightenment, after the assassination of the last Romanoff Czar and his entire family, after the success of the Bolshevik Uprising, news from abroad reported more and continual violent pogroms, unprovoked outbursts of anti-Semitism, not only in the Pale, but also throughout the rest of Europe.

By November 1918, at the close of World War I, in Canada, two opposing poles vied for predominance among the Jewish people in the Ward and in Kensington

Born a Jew...Die a Jew

Market: On the one hand, assimilation into the prosperous, secular world, where unions were being organized, where discussion about social justice ran rampant, and where many immigrants were joining the Canadian peacetime army to stand for freedom. On the other hand, talk of the Zionist dream - the end of *Diaspora* (the dispersion) and a return to the Homeland. This latter group burgeoned with news of the purchase of land in Palestine from the absentee-Arab owners, and subsequent influx of Jewish pioneers settling the land of barren sand dunes, noxious malarial swamps, and rocky wildernesses in their scattered *kibbutzim.*

Older immigrants became engrossed with the myriad possibilities and details of political Zionism, while the younger with families, like Sol, in whom that vision lay dormant, settled down in their Canadian *shtetls* and concerned themselves with their own problems: labor, business and their socialistic goals.

In 1919, the Chernoffs moved into their second home at 54 Denison Avenue, the house where Moshe (Moses), later simply called Marty, was born, on April 4, 1920. Later Samuel was born there too.

For a short time, Sol was drawn into the factories where he learned to modernize his trade by making whole suits from piece work. But, because of the long hours, low pay, and the unhealthy working conditions, in 1921he left the factory and became an independent tailor, owning his own suit store, with his own inventory.

Life for the Canadian immigrant was a never-ending stream of adaptations, both conscious and unconscious, of old ways to new situations; and, in the transition, many families disintegrated.

By 1927, for the Jewish immigrants, conflict at home was firmly entrenched - conflicts between the parents'

The Long Journey

old ways and the enticing new ways of the modern world which interested the children. School teachers, for example, demanded nationalistic loyalty from their students to Canada and Canadian ways. This often conflicted with the children's loyalty to their traditional families and their Jewishness.

At school, children were subtly encouraged to prove how much different, how much better they were than their own parents - to speak, to act and to think differently. For example, there was merit for proper English well spoken, and punishment for lapsing into Yiddish. At home, Yiddish prevailed. Although English was tolerated, it was often scorned. Sadly, many of the students soon began to regard their parents as uneducated, incompetent, or both. For children of the Jewish immigrants, such pressures at school undermined the authority of home, of parents, and of the family's concept of God. Soon, the public-school system had successfully weaned most of the immigrants' children away from their parents.

Sports competitions widened the gap. To Canadian educators, sports provided for clean competition and rehearsal for leadership roles, fair play, team effort, and healthy bodies. To the immigrants, sports, per se, were amusements for the lazy. While Sol tirelessly plied his needles trade, his boys, still very young, also worked. Sometimes they helped in the family tailoring business, but they also sold newspapers on the streets, and often assisted the local Jewish doctors in their offices.

Eventually, with all the pressing aspects of the New World crowding in around them, Sol and Yelena, like many of their friends, and, no doubt, with pressure from their children, decided .to Anglicize most of the family first names: Yelena became Helen, Israel became Irving, Yaacov became Jack, Moshe became Martin (Marty), and

Samuel became Smitty. Rose and Sophie remained Rose and Sophie. The family name was unchanged.

Martin, by age eight, was already street-wise. He had tried and abandoned smoking, and had already worked for pay for two years, but it was a time of confusion. The melting-pot aspects of assimilation versus Helen and Sol's determination to maintain their children's Jewishness thoroughly confused him. He found the teachings of the *heder* confusing. The fact that the harsh rabbi punished the boys for every slight imperfection in reading Hebrew or for ignorance of an obscure Talmudic law, didn't help.

He shrugged off this confusion. He had his own thoughts. He had tasted freedom and wanted more. He wanted freedom from religion, including freedom from his parents' God.

At the same time, Marty had become irresistibly attracted by the sights and sounds of the Christians' holidays, especially by the Ukrainian Catholics' indoor Christmas trees. He used to walk slowly back and forth past their houses, looking in through their windows at the lights and ornaments, and longing to celebrate Christmas at his own home. That subject, of course, was forbidden.

But not the subject of the Pale. Always, always, on every side, he could not escape hearing the interminable, heart-rending stories of life in the Pale. Some immigrants clung to them obsessively, continually telling and retelling stories of life in the Pale, how it was for them there, trying to observe the traditions while wondering where God was during the pogroms, the persecutions, the senseless orgies of violence. Parents and grandparents repeated the stories over and over, to remind all their children and grandchildren, again and again, that those things really did happen.

The Long Journey

Others, trying to divorce themselves from their memories and their European ways, never ever spoke of them again. Among these were Sol and Helen Chernoff, who were hoping to give their children a fresh new identity, Jewish and Canadian at the same time.

Eventually, Marty's struggle with his new identity brought him into contact with a new group of people who would change the course of his life permanently.

CHAPTER THREE

RUNNING FROM GOD

Where can I escape Thy Spirit, or where can I flee from Thy presence? Psalm 139:7

1928-1940: TORONTO, MUSKOKA LAKE

Among the many Jewish people in Toronto were Morris and Ida Kaminsky, directors of the Nathaniel Institute, a Christian outreach to immigrants. The Nathaniel Institute functioned as a community center, offering all types of activities for Jewish immigrants: English classes, Boy Scouts, Sunday school, nursery school, handicraft classes, fellowship, and, as its biggest undertaking of all, the ten-week Summer Camp on Sparrow Lake in the Muskoka Lake region.

On the streets of Marty's neighborhood the children began talking about attending Summer Camp. Only $3.00 for the entire summer! Basketball, volleyball, sleeping in tents, fishing, and best of all, escape from the streets and the rigors of immigrant life in the harsh streets of the Canadian *shtetl.*

Marty, Jack and Smitty begged their mother to let them go. Even their transportation would be provided by the Institute. But Helen was adamant against it. "No!" she said. "The people who run the camp, those Kaminskys, call themselves Jewish Christians! They are *meshumids* (apostates)! No! You are not going!"

In the end, the arguments of the three boys prevailed.

Still opposed, Helen finally gave in and even paid for their camping experience. "Go to camp, enjoy the woods, but" she warned, "don't listen to the *meshumids* and their talk of *Yeska* (a derogatory term for Jesus)!"

And so, at Nathaniel Camp, Marty and his brothers played ball, swam in the lake, and did all the things kids love to do at camp. Marty soon came to love the God-fearing Kaminskys (affectionately called the "Kays"), who, in turn, were full of loving concern for all their little charges. By the end of his first summer at camp, Marty had also learned to love the Word of God.

The Kays became especially fond of Marty, whom they saw as fun-loving, even though somewhat shy and backward. They believed that God's hand was heavy on him, that there was a special call on his life, and they began praying for God's perfect will to be fulfilled in his future. Marty may have been shy, but he was also tough and stubborn. He wanted forgiveness of his sins, eternal life, a relationship with God, and His help to succeed in life, but he did not want to yield his heart to God or to be changed by the Spirit of God.

Year after year, long after his two brothers lost interest, Marty continued to go, every summer, to Nathaniel Camp, and to attend classes during the winter at the Institute.

Meanwhile, the Boom of the 20s, the Depression of the 30s, and the War years of the early 40s were good to Sol Chernoff. His business prospered. In the 20s, he and two other Jewish businessmen opened a clothes factory, calling it Canadian Clothiers. In the 30s, he sold his share of the business to the other partners and started his own business, by opening two men's clothing stores - Field's and Irwin's. A third store was opened sometime in the 40s. When other prospering immigrants moved northwards toward the area of College and Dundas Streets,

Running From God

Sol also moved his family out of Kensington Market and, eventually, to 69 Grace Street, ever nearer to the Nathaniel Institute.

Marty attended both public school and *heder* until he was twelve, but although Helen had saved her money for Marty's *bar mitzvah,* he refused to participate, as did his other brothers. He continued to live outwardly as a secular atheistic Jew, but he spent many hours at the Nathaniel Institute, especially impressed by the believers' obvious love for him and for one another, and their hearty handshakes. No one anywhere ever had grasped his hand like they did!

In Nathaniel's Upper Room, Marty could study *Torah* (the five Books of Moses) and parts of the *Brit Hadashah* (New Covenant) uninterrupted, and he learned much about *Yeshua.* He loved spending time with Jewish believers, singing spiritual songs (often in Yiddish), memorizing Scripture verses, and sharing fellowship suppers and *noshes* (snacks).

Throughout his teens, he served as a counselor for younger boys at Summer Camp, eating and sleeping with them, and helping them chop wood, and burn garbage. Once he and another young Jewish believer knelt by the cot of the senior counselor, Ed Brotsky, who was suffering terribly from poison ivy. The two boys prayed for Ed's healing, and God miraculously relieved him. From then on, Marty knew without a doubt that God answered prayer, and he continually encouraged others to pray for their needs. In his day-to-day living, however, Marty had little time for God. He loved sports and excelled at them, but he also worked long, hard hours after school to help with the family finances. Some day he would be free to live as he wanted, but for now he was too busy to serve God.

Once Marty literally came face-to-face with his Maker.

Born a Jew...Die a Jew

In a public swimming pool he took in too much water and was drowning. His body cramped. He felt like lead and began to sink. In a panic, he kicked up to the surface and called out for help, but no one heard him. With his mouth and nose full of water, and going under for what he felt was the last time, in desperation he cried out as best he could, "God, help me!" Somehow he remembered hearing an audible voice: "Raise your hand, and you will be saved."

Close to blacking out, Marty thrust his right hand above the water. Someone, he never found out who, grabbed his hand and pulled him up and out of the water onto the side of the pool, where he sat choking and gasping, until he finally gained his breath and looked around. There was no one there. He never did learn who it was who pulled him out of the pool that day. He felt that God had saved him. Still, he was not ready to yield everything to God and hardened his heart against his Creator.

Meanwhile, the world was fast spinning toward another cataclysmic war. Trouble for Jewish people was nothing new. For a generation, while Western Europe and the rest of the "civilized" world basked in the illusion of peace, a new Aryan racism was being birthed by French and German philosophers, resurrecting Nietzsche's nineteenth-century call for an Aryan supernation, purged of its Christian and Jewish "slave mentality." By 1900 many professing Christians believed that God Himself was punishing the Jewish people as "Christ-killers," while others were openly jealous of their successes in every field in an otherwise "Christianized" world.

After Germany's humiliating defeat in World War I, life within her borders deteriorated, and anti-Semitism grew proportionately. Jewish people fled their homes

Running From God

whenever and wherever they could find an open door. Thousands fled to Palestine, but by 1929 the government of Great Britain, wielding the authority of the Mandate over Palestine, delegated to it by the League of Nations, closed that door as well.

The new terror in Germany culminated in the ascension to power of an obscure painter from Austria whose name was Adolf Hitler. By 1933, as chancellor of Germany, he began rearming the nation. By 1934, having disenfranchised all Germany's Jews, he took away their businesses and professions. While Jewish people sought frantically for any means of escape, thousands were arrested and shipped to concentration camps. By 1935, Jewish people could not even buy their way out of Germany. Those who did manage to escape had the doors of other countries slam in their faces, including those of the United States, England, Canada, and several South American nations.

Because of self-interest and ambition, fueled by Arab threats to cut off their oil supply, the British did not want Palestine to become a Jewish homeland. As one writer described the period, "Hitler chased the Jewish people out, and the British sealed them in - to their deaths."

Though all of Europe ignited in the flames of war, nothing stopped the brutal orgy of bloodlust set in motion by the Nazis, who wore the Crusader Cross on their uniforms. Before the outbreak of the Second World War there were nearly nine million Jewish people living in the country villages, provincial towns, and large metropolitan centers throughout Europe. Seven years later, in Greece, Holland, Hungary, White Russia, the Ukraine, Belgium, Yugoslavia, Rumania and Norway, over 50 percent had vanished. In Czechoslovakia, 85 percent. In Poland, Estonia, Latvia, Lithuania, Germany and Austria:, 90 percent had disappeared.

But these are only statistics. The slaughtered Jews did not all die in Nazi-held territories. During the British blockade of Palestine's ports, the overcrowded refugee boat *Patria* was blown up within sight of Haifa Harbor. There were no survivors. The leaky, overladen, old wooden ship *Struma* sank at sea (no survivors). Sometimes at night, when illegal rescue ships managed to run the blockade, members of the Israeli underground *Haganah* met the refugees in the surf, handed them down from the old boat, crowded them into smaller boats or rafts, and then shoved them ashore. At other times, they passed the weakest ones from hand-to-hand through the surf to the dry land. Always, groups of Zionists and *kibbutzniks* (settlers) waited in the shadows with dry clothes and "papers," then spirited the new arrivals straight to the *kibbutzim.*

Sometimes they were caught. When alerted English soldiers intercepted the blockade runner *Exodus,* they dragged the more than five-thousand screaming, weeping, pleading refugees straight to another ship. One ancient old man wrested himself free just long enough to kneel down and kiss the soil. Some died of heart attacks. The British shipped them back to the same detention camp on Cyprus from which they had come.

Marty tried to ignore the reports of the War raging in Europe. He also tried to ignore the Kays, who kept presenting Messianic prophecy to him from the *Tanach,* in particular the Suffering Servant of Isaiah 53. He tried to ignore the words, but he could not get them out of his mind:

> *He was despised and shunned by men, a man of sufferings and acquainted with sickness; and we hid our faces at the sight of Him; He was despised and we did not esteem Him. Surely He has borne our sicknesses*

Running From God

and carried our sorrows; yet we regarded Him as a stricken one, smitten of God, and afflicted. But He was pierced for our transgressions; He was bruised for our iniquities; the punishment which procured our peace fell upon Him, and with His stripes we are healed. All we like sheep have gone astray; we have turned each one to his own way; and the Lord has laid on Him the iniquity of us all.

He was maltreated, and He submitted Himself; He opened not His mouth; as a lamb that is led to the slaughter and as a sheep before her shearers is dumb, so He opened not His mouth. From distress and from judgment He was taken, and who of His contemporaries would consider that He was cut off from the land of the living for the transgressions of my covenant people to whom the stroke was due?

Isaiah 53:3-8

The words stuck with him, haunted him, and he could not resolve in his mind who this might be. Had he not read for himself the description of the man punished for the sins of the world, he would not have believed it. He could not deny in his head that *Yeshua* of Nazareth was doubtless Messiah, but still he ref used to accept it in his heart.

He also tried to ignore the "still, small voice" calling him to surrender his heart and his life to God. Like his father before him, he knew that if he surrendered his life to *Yeshua* he would not only be changed, separated from his sinful street life, but also alienated from his family. He thought he might even cause the death of his own mother, and was sure that surrender to Jesus meant giving himself in service for the Messiah for as long as he would live. And that he fought with all his being.

Born a Jew...Die a Jew

In 1940, when Marty was twenty years old, God began once more pressing him for a decision.

Still painfully shy, Marty borrowed a book from a neighbor, *How To Win Friends and Influence People,* by Dale Carnegie. Strangely, the book gave him a hunger to know more about God, so next he borrowed a Bible from the same man. He took the Bible home and began to read it secretly. He did not want his family to find it, and he also did not want the praying Kays and the others at Nathaniel Institute to know that he was once again studying the Bible, this time at home.

Again, God brought him to the point of decision, and again he found it difficult to yield. Miserable and restless, like Jonah fleeing from God, he tried to run away. He left town for a tailoring job in Montreal, Quebec, unaware as he boarded the train, that two intercessors in Toronto were prompted by God to spend that same night in fasting and prayer for his salvation.

By the time he reached Montreal he was so miserable, he knew he could no longer resist the Messiah and live. Returning home to Toronto, he went straight to the Nathaniel Institute, fell on his knees, and prayed with his faithful friend and mentor, Morris Kaminsky, asking God for forgiveness for his sins and for eternal life in Messiah. The heaviness lifted. The restlessness and tension left. He rose from his knees, confident that he was born-again, a new man in Messiah, a bond servant of *Yeshua.* Old things had passed away; all things were new; and Marty Chernoff was filled with joy.

Chapter Four

A Stranger In A Strange Land

The Lord said to Abram: As for you, leave your land, your relatives and your father's household for a land which I will show you. Genesis 12:1

1940-1949: Toronto, the Carolinas, Atlanta

What Marty had suspected was true: His life would never be the same once he accepted *Yeshua* as Savior. He suddenly hungered to know the whole Word of God, gulping down huge Scripture portions, memorizing chapters, even entire books of the *Brit Hadasha*. In company with his friends, Ed Brotsky, Dan Rogers, and other Jewish believers, he reveled in the many Bible studies led by Mr. Kay at the Institute. Very early in his experience he began leading children's groups, teaching them to love Bible stories, and to sing spiritual songs. The children loved him in return. Completely serious and dedicated to his calling, he never lost any of his ability to have fun with children. He knew how to pray, but he never forgot how to play.

Marty, from the beginning of his experience with *Yeshua*, was a soul winner, leading many of his young charges at Summer Camp and a number of his close, personal friends, as well, to a saving knowledge of the Lord. But, sadly, there on the sidelines stood his beloved, spiritually-blinded family.

He had always been very tender towards his mother and was extremely concerned about how both his parents would react when he told them about his faith in *Yeshua*. Rose had come home one afternoon and shocked everyone by announcing that she intended to marry a non-Jewish boy from the neighborhood. Helen was dumbstruck, and Sol, in a fit of temper, beat Rose severely. Then he told her to get out and never return. After she left, they had said *kaddish* (the Jewish prayer for the dead) over her, and tried to forget her.

Marty felt he could not bear a weight of rejection such as they had heaped upon Rose, but he also knew he could not remain silent forever. Remaining silent would be to deny *Yeshua* before them and before the angels of God. After much prayer and fasting before the Lord on his part, and continually bathed in prayer for mercy by his friends at the Institute, as gently as he could, Marty tried on several occasions to share his faith with his parents. Each time he did this, Sol remained strangely silent, avoiding Marty's eyes, while Helen became hysterical, screaming and crying and, once, crashing her hand through a window, threatening to bleed to death in front of them all.

"What else can happen to me! Nothing! This is the worst!" she cried to the heavens. "My daughter is dead. Now my son tells me he is a traitor! It is time for me to die and get this life over and done with!"

Emboldened by the Kays' encouragement to witness wherever he was, Marty was able to stand firm while his entire family threatened to disown him. When they saw his determination, they eventually relented. Helen did not commit suicide, and the family did not disown him or say kaddish over him. Rose, however, never returned home, and, sadly, the family lost touch with her altogether.

A Stranger In A Strange Land

While waiting his turn to be drafted into the Canadian Army, Marty attended Moody Bible Institute in Chicago, Illinois, for six months. While there, he had two profound experiences.

First, he read Charles Finney's book, *Revival Lectures*. The impact the book made on him was stunning. Even though he had been a born-again believer for three years, serving as youth leader at Summer Camp, winning souls to the Lord, and suffering persecution for his efforts, he suddenly realized that, even though he had asked God for forgiveness, he had never experienced the same conviction of sin accompanied by deep repentance leading to the regeneration that Finney had written about. He now gained a deeper understanding of the areas of his life that needed spiritual attention.

Under a crushing fear that maybe he was not completely delivered after all, and with throbbing remorse, he fell on his knees, weeping, confessing and repenting of all of his sins on every level - one-by-one. This time, he saw and accepted the absolute necessity of the Lord's death and resurrection for the cleansing of his soul, realizing in the deepest reaches of his spirit his total dependence upon God alone for his very breath. This time he painfully obeyed the Scriptural admonition:

> *That you are to rid yourself of the old nature with your previous habits ... and that you put on the new nature that is created in God's likeness.*
>
> Ephesians 4:22, 24

Marty had just experienced a deep work of commitment and sanctification to the God of Israel that he had never experienced before. It confirmed to him that the Messiah's work of atonement was completed within him forever. Bursting with joy and flooded with peace, he began thirsting for the power of the Holy Spirit, hungering for the power of revival.

But the Canadian Army called, and Marty was inducted on June 11, 1942. When he reported to boot camp, he was put in charge of giving the new recruits their gear and uniforms. With a holy, hidden agenda and *hutzpah* to match, Marty presented himself like a surly sergeant, snapping at the new recruits one-by-one:

"What's your name?"

"John Jones, sir."

"Where are you from?"

"Toronto, sir."

"Are you saved? Are you born-again?"

"Well, I dunno, sir."

"Report to me tonight for Bible study in the barracks!"

"Yessir!"

Marty was a bold witness in the army, although it brought him persecution there too. He held a Bible study and led many young soldiers to knowledge, repentance and salvation in the Lord.

By the end of his tour of duty, having served both his country and his Lord honorably, he was still only twenty-two years old. Discharged on November 2, 1943, he returned to Toronto. Sol had suffered a stroke and needed constant care, so Marty lived at home to support his mother and help care for his father.

At the same time, with his burning desire to know and to understand the entire Bible, he decided to attend Toronto Baptist Bible College. There was no Messianic Movement, no Messianic *Yeshivas* (Bible schools) or even Messianic Judaism. So the only place for a Jewish believer in *Yeshua* to go, therefore, to learn more of the Bible was a Christian Bible school. Marty knew that his attendance at such an institution could cause negative repercussions in his family, and it did. It was especially of-

A Stranger In A Strange Land

fensive to his sister Sophie. Every time he left the house, he had to carry all his religious school books and papers with him because she would burn anything he left behind.

One day, while Marty was home alone with his father, to his surprise and great joy, Sol confessed his secret, that for twenty years, ever since his days of attending Rev. Rohold's meetings, he too had been a secret believer in *Yeshua*. Marty was thrilled. After sharing with Sol what he had learned about repentance, Marty had the incomparable privilege of leading his own father in a prayer of repentance and salvation. Six months later, Sol suffered a second stroke that carried him home to his Savior and Lord.

Meanwhile, Marty had been feeling a growing desire for an even deeper, more intimate walk with the Lord. He kept reading more and more in the Word about a wondrous experience, a second blessing, about which he was not being taught at the seminary - being filled with the Holy Spirit and with fire. The Kays, who had some knowledge of others having had such an experience, confessed to being wary of what they called "wildfire," a manifestation of the Holy Spirit that sometimes seemed to get out of control. Happily, about this time, someone else came into Marty's life who held the key. At New Covenant House on College Street, Marty met Earl Bruneau, who instructed him about this work of the Holy Spirit, and the ensuing Spirit-filled life. Profoundly affected by Bruneau's teachings, Marty was himself filled with the Holy Spirit. He was so on fire for God that, although he had not yet experienced speaking in tongues, he often stayed up the whole night in prayer.

With the end of World War II in the summer of 1945, the horror of the European Holocaust began to break upon the world. Fifty million people had died, six million of them Jews, in ditches, death camps and gas ovens. It now became known to a shocked world that Hitler's scientists had experimented with live humans, often wrenching sex organs from unanesthetized patients; that his mistress Eva Braun, with whom he committed suicide, had commissioned lamp shades made from human skin; that children had been · torn in half, babies' heads bashed against the walls, young girls raped and murdered before their parents' eyes. The Nazi nightmare of horrors, against the Jews and against European civilization in general, had exceeded the cruelties of the ancient Romans. The world would never be the same.

With an overwhelming burden for his stricken people everywhere, especially for his mother and his siblings, to experience the glorious liberty in their Messiah, shy Marty - never shy when talking about his Lord - often went alone door-to-door and store-to-store after school, spreading the Good News of the Savior. Yelena could avoid the subject only by looking the other way.

Although he never received a theological degree, he studied extensively at Moody Bible Institute, Toronto Bible School, and Toronto Baptist Seminary. He rejected the intellectual approach to faith and witnessing in favor of being a lay-minister, a revivalist, a frontline soul-winner led by the Holy Spirit with power. Through Earl Bruneau's influence, he decided to seek "letters from no man." He was being trained by the Lord Himself, though often feeling that he walked alone. He yearned for God's specific will for his life, even if that meant having to leave home and live a celibate life.

In 1948, Marty received a letter from his Canadian friend, Arthur Glass, an older Jewish believer who was working in the United States with the Southern Witness to Israel (SWI), an outreach based in Chattanooga, Tennessee. He invited Marty to join him in sharing *Yeshua*

A Stranger In A Strange Land

as the Messiah with the Jewish people in the Carolinas. Thrilled by the invitation, Marty told his mother, his family and, especially, his friends at Nathaniel Institute and New Covenant House good-bye, closed his suitcase, and left Toronto to live the rest of his life in the United States. He had embarked on what was to become the goal of his life's call: working for the salvation of his own people and the restoration of Israel as a nation.

As Marty worked closely with Arthur and the SWI, his vision and love for his people increased. Living quietly in one room, he spent much time alone in prayer. Riding the circuit on buses and trains throughout the Carolinas, he preached in churches, Bible study groups, and wherever else there was an open door. While leading many to salvation, he helped organize thirteen "Wild Olive Prayer Groups" among non-Jews who had a love and burden for the Jewish people, and hearts to intercede and support the formation of a homeland for them in Palestine.

Meanwhile, by 1948, even after the full horror of the War became known, Europe was still fertile ground for further scape-goating of the Jews for a nation's failing economy and high unemployment. Marty felt strongly that Christians had not cared enough about what was happening to the Jewish people during the threatening years leading up to World War II, nor been concerned enough during the War years to deter the Holocaust. He knew that God cared, and life was now again becoming increasingly intolerable for the Jews in Europe.

More burdened than ever before, for Jews at home and abroad, he travailed in prayer for a move of God's Holy Spirit in revival among His people everywhere. Teaching and preaching at every open door, he spread himself too thin. The geographical area he tried to cover

Born a Jew...Die a Jew

was too vast for one man. So, when a number of businessmen from Atlanta, professing deep concern for the salvation of Israel, encouraged Marty to move to Atlanta and make it the hub of his operations, he agreed.

With their verbal promises of support, but with nothing signed and sealed in his hand, he resigned from his salaried position with SWI and moved to Atlanta, into a dreary boarding house, eager to share his vision. The businessmen who had invited him, however, soon lost interest, both in him and in his call, and their promises proved to be empty ones. Inexperienced and totally unequipped to raise support through a newsletter, Marty did know how to pray, and he spent much time on his knees, not only poring over the Scriptures, studying about revival, and praying for the salvation of Israel, but now "walking by faith," trusting God to supply his financial needs.

As he concentrated in prayer, he saw in the Spirit that "the fields were white unto harvest," and that Jewish lives were slipping away into eternity without God. It bothered him, vaguely at first, that there were no special places for born-again Jews to fellowship with other Jewish believers except in denominational churches, where they soon became assimilated and lost their cultural identity.

Marty grieved, realizing that the expectation among most Christians was for large numbers of Jewish people to be saved only during the prophetic seven-year Great Tribulation Period preceding the Messiah's return to this earth when the AntiMessiah (AntiChrist) would rule the world. Some believers felt that Jewish people would only be saved when the Messiah returned to reign. Because of this "small-remnant mentality," no one was even talking about the possibility of a Jewish revival happening before then. Then, without trumpet call or angelic warn-

A Stranger In A Strange Land

ing, in the fall of 1948, shortly after Israel became a state, God emblazoned across the sky in front of Marty's eyes the first of his three stunning visions of a coming harvest of Jewish souls:

A vast and endless orchard spread out across the land, fruit trees and vines laden with ripened fruit. The finger of God reached down and stirred the trees and the vines. The leaves began to rustle, and the branches began to shake.

God was showing Marty a great multitude of Jewish people coming to the saving knowledge of the Messiah, and he knew God was calling him to pray for it. He cried out, "God, let me see the fulfillment of this glorious vision." He wept and he praised God for this display of His great love and compassion for His Jewish people everywhere. He prayed constantly, from then on, for the Lord of the harvest to raise up more and more and more harvesters, and to send them forth into the harvest.

Even while walking in such close affinity with the invisible God of Heaven, however, Marty still often felt the pangs of loneliness and longed to be married. But to marry just to be married would not do for him. He had been taught by the Kays that the wrong mate could destroy what God wanted to accomplish through a life. His wife, therefore, would have to be Jewish, or, at the very least, called to the salvation of the Jewish people. She would have to be given to hospitality, willing to work shoulder-to-shoulder with her husband, and she would have to be someone who knew the importance of prevailing prayer and victory over the self-life that only the Holy Spirit can bring.

It was not that he hadn't looked for such a person. Marty had, from time to time, suffered much discouragement seeking the right mate. Few Jewish girls were getting saved, and even fewer non-Jewish girls were being called to the Jewish people. Perhaps the wife his heart longed for did not even exist, he thought. With his whole heart, he wanted to draw ever closer to God, and if that meant that he might have to walk alone, he was willing to do that. He was a stranger in a strange land, and his face was set as a flint. He would walk all the way alone, by faith, if that was the will of his Lord.

Then, one day, when he was twenty-nine years old, he received a letter in the mail that changed the course of his life once again. It was from me. I was writing from Knoxville, Tennessee, inviting him to the University of Tennessee to share his testimony and his vision with Jewish student friends of mine who I knew would be receptive to what he had to say. He could stay near campus with a member of the UT chapter of InterVarsity Student Fellowship, and I would cover his transportation costs and other expenses.

Marty prayed about the letter. He believed his correspondent to be an older woman with a ministry of intercession for Jewish students, so he decided to enter through this door of opportunity to share the Good News of the Messiah with her friends. It was a comforting feeling that afterward he could safely leave any new believers in her capable hands.

Chapter Five

My Own Search

Do not recall former events, nor consider longer the things of the past. Behold, I do a new thing; now it is springing forth ... .   Isaiah 43:18-19

You shall then be called by a new name which the mouth of the Lord shall bestow.   Isaiah 62:2

1930-1946: Knoxville

In June of 1930, socially and culturally far and away from the hustle and bustle of the frenetic and exciting Jewish centers of Toronto, in Knoxville, Tennessee, an ultra-liberal, high-Methodist minister christened me Joanna Joyner. My early years in that small city on the banks of the Tennessee River were fairly uneventful. My father, a doctor who worked for the state, traveled. My mother owned a successful employment agency. In 1938, they quietly divorced.

Four years after the divorce, when I was almost twelve, Mother became engaged to a highly-prominent, wonderful man, and I began making plans to attend Winston-Salem Academy, the finishing school which a number of my girlfriends in our social circle would attend. Two years later, however, when Mother's fiancé died suddenly of a heart attack, I decided to live at home with her, and attend the University of Tennessee instead.

Mother and I never argued. If she did not like what I

did, she became sick. Even though all her relatives were from hardy stock, she was frequently ailing, and no doctor had ever been able to successfully diagnose just what was wrong with her. This they communicated to me, so I always suspected that her illnesses were, at least in part, a result of emotional stress.

A number of Jewish professionals and students lived and worked in our neighborhood near the university campus. At first they were largely invisible to me, because at home it was considered unseemly to discuss either race or religion. Politics, on the other hand, was an acceptable subject - since we were all active Democrats.

Longing for a cause, at about the age of 15, I turned to politics and, in my high school, I organized the first Democratic High School Youth Group in the country. Mostly what we did was hold youth rallies, serve at banquets, make phone calls, usher at political meetings, and meet important people, including President Franklin D. Roosevelt. That was exciting, but politics did not satisfy me. I was searching for something to which I could make a lifetime commitment.

Mother had raised me in a formal, high-society, Methodist church, spending much money, time and effort grooming me for the future, expecting me to fulfill her dreams of marrying, not necessarily wealth, but at least status. Since I was fully expected to exemplify polite society, to be active at the country club, to function within a semi-closed social group, to center my activities around sororities and dance classes, piano lessons, and charity work for church and community, she and my usually-absent father introduced me to society at an informal coming-out dance when I was barely sixteen.

I loved my many good friends and my church family. I now remember the sermons as promoting a social gos-

My Own Search

pel, but God Himself always seemed close to me from the age of twelve, and I prayed to Him often, trusting Him to help me do well in school.

One evening, at a Methodist Youth Conference in another state, I heard God speak directly into my heart during the vesper service. Startled, I realized I had heard no audible words, but I knew positively that God Himself had called me to serve Him full-time. Down on my knees at the altar, during the consecration service of the final day, deep within my heart, but with no real understanding of what it meant, I committed my life to God for His service.

Back home, facing two months of summer vacation, I set aside every early afternoon to read my Bible and the books I had bought at the conference bookstore and to pray. Nothing new happened - or so it seemed to me. The Scriptures were closed to me. The books seemed frivolous. When I prayed, God seemed farther away than ever, although I could feel my love for Him growing.

One day I knelt beside my bed. Assuming God could hear me, I told Him all about it. I said, "God, if there is something standing between us, please let me know what it is. I feel that there is some kind of wall separating us, and I don't know what to do about it."

Again, nothing happened - or so it seemed.

At a later conference, I was again confronted by the call of the Lord, this time to foreign service, "no matter how sacrificial, how unpleasant, or where it might lead," the speaker warned.

Sacrificial? Unpleasant? What about my dreams, Mother's dreams of my marrying prestige and wealth, of settling down in a beautiful home, raising beautiful children, and living luxuriously and happily ever after with my Prince Charming - whom I was yet to meet? This time, the struggle with my imagination and my will intensified, as I envisioned rancid, steaming jungles, pestilential wells and garbage-strewn streets in emerging, undeveloped nations, festering, disease-ridden natives, surrounded by knotty-kneed, balloon-bellied, naked children. Alone, I wrestled all day in the spirit, missing meals, while my imagination ran wild. Did I really prefer God to the comforts and riches of my dreams?

Finally, when I tried to picture a life of high society without God's friendship and approval, I saw how desolate, how barren it would be for me. The alternative to following God, wherever He might lead me, would be a life without purpose. This thought led me to surrender all to Him.

Not my will, but Thine be done.   Luke 22:42

Despite this new experience with God, once I got home I was grieved that the elusive, spiritual barrier still stood, separating me from my Savior. "God," I pleaded, "please, show me what it is and what to do about it." My words seemed to be in vain, rebounding from the ceiling and returning to me as so much noise.

No matter how much I tried I could not seem to bridge the gap between God and myself. I did not know what was wrong and why I was missing the mark in my relationship with the Lord.

Dan Miller, a former boyfriend of mine, and fraternity student, a sophisticated intellectual who had gone to college to study classical piano, called me a week later and wanted to see me. He had something important to say.

He took me canoeing, and when we got to the middle of the river, he suddenly put up the paddle and said, "Joanna, a wonderful thing has happened to me. I have

My Own Search

accepted Jesus as my Savior. Listen to this," and he pulled a small Bible out of his shirt pocket and began to read:

> *All we like sheep have gone astray; we have turned each one to his own way; and the Lord has laid on Him the iniquity of us all.* Isaiah 53:6

"On *Him,*" he said. "That's Jesus. Listen." And he continued reading selected Scriptures:

> *There is none righteous, not even one.*
> Romans 3:10

> *For God did not send His Son into the world to condemn the world, but in order that the world that the world might be saved through Him.* John 3:17

> *If we confess our sins, He is faithful and just to forgive us our sins and to cleanse us from all unrighteousness.* 1 John 1:9

"Joanna," he said, "Jesus came to earth to forgive me for all my sins, and He died for me on the cross, so that I could live with Him forever. He wants to do the same for you."

He stared at me eagerly, and I stared back at him. What was he talking about? In spite of my religiosity and all the experiences I had that summer, I still did not understand. I did see that Dan was not the same person he had been. Until that moment, I had been so sure I was the only person within my circle of friends with a compelling thirst for the knowledge of God, and it startled me to hear him talking about Jesus intimately and with excitement and confidence. If nothing else it made me envious. When he invited me to attend InterVarsity Christian Fellowship's summer Bible studies with him, I eagerly accepted.

To my amazement, the InterVarsity Bible studies were attended by many intensely-joyous young people, excited about their relationship with God through Jesus. How enthusiastically they sang! How confidently they prayed! How intimately they praised the eternal God! How unashamedly they loved one another! I was fascinated.

As I continued to attend the meetings, the Word of God became alive to me. Jesus the Savior became real and personal. God Himself was, indeed, among them.

One evening, soon after my sixteenth birthday, a few of us attended a little Open Bible Church where the Book of Revelation was being taught, along with other relevant Scriptures. There I heard for the first time about a coming falling away of believers in the Last Days, and the rise of cold, liberal churches with a form of godliness but a denial of the true power of God.

Suddenly, I understood the barrier: I had never been "born-again" by God's Spirit. The Good News of salvation, that the shed blood of Jesus alone cleanses from all sin, was not being preached from the pulpit of the church that held my membership. In its place, a social gospel of works and politics had been substituted. No wonder I had not understood what God wanted from me! He wanted repentance from sin and acceptance of His Son's sacrificial death as payment for those sins.

That night, I was finally born into the Kingdom of God. The barrier fell, and it all became clear to me. From then on, my prayer and study times were wonderfully exciting, because Jesus of Nazareth, the Son of God, was

My Own Search

the Savior of the world, and alive and well. More importantly, He was also alive and well in my heart - at last!

Little did I realize the dramatic changes this spiritual transformation would reap in my life in the very near future.

Chapter Six

A Twentieth-Century Ruth

The foreigners who join themselves to the Lord, to minister to Him, to love the name of the Lord, and to be His servants ... them I will bring to My holy mountain, and I will make them joyful in My house of prayer. ... Thus says the Lord God, who gathers the exiles of Israel, I will collect others unto them besides those already gathered.   Isaiah 56:6-8

1946-1949: Knoxville

By the fall of 1946, my life had changed completely. Though I was hardly aware of its happening, my old friends and social groups no longer held my interest. They were gradually being replaced by new friends from InterVarsity Fellowship. Contributing unintentionally to my loving mother's dire consternation, I began choosing my friends for their level of spirituality, rather than for their social standing. When she realized what direction I was going, she worried in earnest.

As long as I dated InterVarsity boys in good standing within our social circle, she was unconcerned. But when I turned down invitations to dances and country-club affairs, devoting myself instead to my new friends, attending prayer meetings, teaching Sunday school at the nearby Crippled Children's Hospital, but not attending her church, she became very vocal. Lowering her voice, she spoke scornfully to me, "You are going too far,

Joanna! Your new friends are religious fanatics, and you're becoming a fanatic!" She was not the only one who thought so. All my relatives and all my long-term spiritual leaders loudly rejected my new "fanaticism."

While still president of my Methodist Youth Group, I was bringing in leaders from InterVarsity and the Baptist Student Union to speak to our handful of members on Sunday evenings. When they began teaching what the Bible says about heaven and hell, and praying with the young people to accept the Lord, attendance climbed into the hundreds. At these packed meetings, 80 percent of the unsaved young people who attended made professions of faith.

When the pastor heard about it, he was furious and summoned me to his study. In a rage, he forbade me to teach a "butcher's religion" of blood sacrifice in his church. He forbade me to teach the Bible as the Word of God. He declared that one day they would dig up the bones of Jesus of Nazareth in Palestine! I was shocked. He was, in fact, saying that he believed that Jesus was no more than a human being, one who never rose from the dead at all!

At the same time, some of my friends from InterVarsity and I were still occasionally attending an Open Bible Church. When I also began sharing what we were learning there with the Methodist young people, I was told in no uncertain terms that my authority with them was rescinded, and my activities within the group thereby limited. Thus ostracized by my church, I felt that it was time to leave. That touched off the first and final war I had with my mother. When I told her I also wanted, with all my heart, to be immersed in water, she raised her voice to me for the very first time: "Stay away from those people! You were sprinkled when you were a baby! You don't need this! Joanna, you are rejecting your heritage!"

A Twentieth-Century Ruth

In spite of her opposition, deep in my heart I knew what I wanted and what I needed to do. I found a minister who agreed to immerse me over Mother's objections, but she had her lawyer threaten to sue him, so he backed out. This was repeated several times. From her point of view, it was unacceptable to deviate from the traditions of her church and she was willing to go to extremes to keep me from doing it.

In September 1947, after I had been a born-again believer for a year, I enrolled as a freshman at the University of Tennessee, then attended the InterVarsity Conference in Georgia that fall. Only with great persistence had I persuaded Mother to allow me to attend. The conference focused on outreach to foreign countries, and believers from fields of service around the world came and displayed their photographs and their wonderful literature on tables lined up around the walls of the school gym where the conference was held.

I approached one of the speakers and explained to him that I felt called of God for service, but I did not know where. "How could I find out?" I asked him. He suggested that I collect some of the literature from all the fields represented there at the conference, take them home, and pray over them. He assured me that, as I began to pray, God would show me where my call was.

I left the conference loaded with brochures from Asia, India, Africa, Europe, and the islands of the sea. There were also brochures from home missions such as Child Evangelism and InterVarsity Campus Ministries. Once home in my room, I prayed fervently over each one, asking God to show me what He had planned for my life. In response, God began to work by moving a new family into our neighborhood, a young Jewish doctor, his wife and their two very wild little boys.

Roger, the eldest boy, at barely five-years old, soon began visiting me almost every afternoon when I came home from classes. I loved his visits. Baby-sitting and playing with children were my two special interests. Little precocious Roger asked me many questions. One day, when I sat down beside him, to my great joy he hopped onto my lap, took hold of the cross I wore on a chain around my neck, and said, "Tell me this story."

What could I do? I knew only a little about the beliefs of my Jewish neighbors, and I did not want to offend them. I had heard that his parents both claimed to be atheists; but, since little Roger was insistent, I told him the Good News of the Messiah - all of it.

"But why did He die on the cross?" he asked me.

"He died for our sins. For all who believe and invite Him into their heart to be their Savior, He saves them from sin's punishment."

"I believe," he said. "How can I ask Him into my heart?"

"Just bow your head and pray and ask Him," I said; and little Roger bowed his head. We prayed, and he received the Lord into his heart. From that moment on, both our lives were changed.

Shortly thereafter, his mother came over and introduced herself. She knew of the decision Roger had made because there had been an amazing change in his behavior. From being an unmanageable child, he now read Bible stories to his baby brother, and he tried very hard to be good. She thought I would want to know. I was ecstatic!

Sadly, she and her husband both admitted they had ruled God out of their lives and become socialistic. Their home life was volatile, empty and sad. I became very anxious for them, and spent a good deal of time talking with them about the Lord and praying for them.

Her brother, an embittered World War II veteran, moved in with them, and taught me much about the

A Twentieth-Century Ruth

Holocaust, specifically the horrors of Dachau, which he had experienced firsthand. I prayed for him too, that God would heal his memories, and save his soul. I prayed that little Roger would someday plant a seed of truth and life in the dry ground of his heart.

I discovered that many of our other neighbors were also Jewish, as were a number of my personal friends, and I began praying for them, too. While I continued praying round-the-world to see where God might use me, He was already using my time spent with my Jewish neighbors and friends to turn me in the direction I was to take for the rest of my life. Gradually, I realized that all my prayers and emotions had become centered on the Jewish people. Whenever I read the Bible, the words "Israel," "Zion," and "the Jews" seemed to leap out at me from every page, and I would weep and weep, as God burned the Scriptures into my soul and spirit.

From then on, I was single-minded, reading everything I could get my hands on about the Jewish people, their history, and the history and geography of what was then called "Palestine." Like Ruth the Moabitess, I literally became *a ger tzedek* (spiritual convert) to the House of Israel six months before Israel even became a state. I knew by then that I was called to be a servant to the Jewish people, to actually be one with them - whatever that might entail.

I began rediscovering former Jewish friends and shared the Good News with them. I met Jewish men and women students on campus and shared with them. I found many of them very open to the claims of the Savior, although I felt awkward speaking to them from their own Scriptures.

I was so filled with love for the Jewish people, I went to the president of InterVarsity on campus and tried to explain to him my love, my burden, my calling to the children of Israel. He listened quietly, shrugged, and said with a sigh, "Well, there's one thing about the Jews: If you let them in, they'll take over. The medical school in Memphis maintains a quota on Jews, or they'd take over the entire school."

I was shocked at his manner. I had assumed that all true Christians loved all other people; but here was a professing Christian voicing deep-rooted, anti-Semitic prejudice as clearly as the European anti-Semites we were beginning to hear about again in the news. My fresh experiences with God and His chosen people had so profoundly affected me that the shock of this encounter caused me to withdraw emotionally from this man and several other "Christian" friends, who thought as he did.

Fortunately, I had several distinct outlets for my wounded emotions: the Jewish students and friends I had already made on campus, and with whom I discussed Messiah constantly; the Jewish family next door, for whom I baby-sat; and Anna, an older woman, a great prayer warrior, who ran a boarding house near the university, and who felt the same way I did about the Jewish people.

During the winter of 1948-49, I started dropping in on Anna before classes, between classes, and sometimes after classes. We discussed the Jewish people and Bible prophecy, and we spent hours praying together for the Jewish settlers in Palestine who were struggling to survive. We prayed for the birth of the nation of Israel. While researching and writing a term paper for an English class on the United Nations sessions to decide the fate of Palestine, I found myself weeping, my deep desire for identification with the Jewish people intensifying more than ever. I longed for friends my age who could understand and share these feelings.

When a young, student couple, Kurt and Mary Weiss, moved in a few doors from us, I was convinced they

A Twentieth-Century Ruth

were sent to me from God. Kurt, a Jewish graduate student working on his doctorate, had already been a believer in Jesus as his Messiah even when, as a child, he escaped the Holocaust in Germany. The terror still fresh in his mind, he spent many long hours telling me what he could remember about Germany, the Holocaust, and the European Jews. In my mind, I compared him with the doctor's haunted brother-in-law, and once again, I saw the incredible healing that a relationship with Jesus brings to a wounded soul.

Kurt, Mary and I already shared many of the same Jewish friends on campus. When Kurt became the sponsor of a fraternity of liberal, Jewish students, mostly from New York, "pink" and radical in their politics, who enjoyed debating new ideas, our circle of interesting and interested students expanded greatly. In class, I met even more Jewish students, some from a conservative fraternity of wealthy Southerners. Many were intrigued by the many Old Testament prophecies concerning the Messiah.

Some of the Jewish fraternity men were soon reading the Bible, and openly discussing the Good News with us. At that time, I had only been saved a year and a half, and had limited information about the New Testament, and even less knowledge of the Hebrew Scriptures. I could take them only so far. From that point, I did not know what else to do with them.

One day, my Jewish friend Neil said to me, "Joanna, the guys in my fraternity really love to get into controversial subjects. The Holocaust got us to asking some pretty heavy questions, and some of the guys might even be open to Jesus' being the Messiah and to a faith we can really live by. So, if you can find some Jewish guy who believes like you do, we'll invite him to the house and listen to what he has to say." Kurt's fraternity brothers agreed to let the same person present the claims of the Messiah to them at their frat house - if I could find someone. So, in the winter of 1948-49, I began my search.

Meanwhile, something else kept coming up that also changed my life radically. The deeper I dug into the Word of God, the more I began to hunger for a deeper experience with God than I already had. In the early spring, I heard good things about the woman pastor of a Nazarene Church that met near a fish market in a very poor section of town. She was teaching about the Holy Spirit, and a few of us from InterVarsity began attending her services. There we were offered the concept of the "second blessing" from God, that of being "immersed into the Holy Spirit," with emphasis not so much on speaking in tongues, but on absolute and permanent surrender of every aspect of life to God's call.

Every aspect? What a dilemma for me! There was one major aspect of my life that I was not ready to surrender, and that was my right to be married, to have a husband and children, and a home of my own. Wrestling in my heart with that deep personal desire all day and all night for almost an entire week, I finally let it go and laid my all on the altar, including my right to be married - if marriage was not the Lord's will for me. It was the hardest decision I ever faced, but I yielded. As soon as I did, I was suddenly overwhelmed with glory, recognizing the experience as the second work of the Holy Spirit, as He literally poured Himself into my spirit. From that moment on, even without the manifestation of tongues, prayer to God and intercession on behalf of all people, especially the Jewish people, blessed me with joy as never before. Then suddenly, gently, lovingly, the Lord graciously confirmed within my spirit that it was indeed His perfect will for me to marry.

I had too much love and respect for my mother to hide anything from her, but perhaps I should not have

A Twentieth-Century Ruth

told her about this experience immediately. She was appalled. "Keep that trashy group from that fish-market church away from here!" she warned me. "I will not let them in this house!"

It grieved me that she felt that way. At the same time, I could not deny that the experience had deepened my love for God and His Word, and for her.

As a young adult, I began to realize that, if the Lord did want me to marry, the choice of my future mate was of prime concern to Him. I wanted only to honor and please Him. From the time I first accepted Jesus as my personal Savior, I knew I could never be interested in anyone, no matter how charming or exciting he might be, unless he shared my call to full-time service. Since the winter of 1947-48, I began to feel so absorbed, so "converted" to the Jewish people, that the idea of marriage to someone not Jewish seemed totally unacceptable to me. Now, after having been filled with the Holy Spirit, I knew that I could never marry anyone who had not also had that experience. Then, as I was in prayer one day, the Lord assured me that my future mate would be a Jewish believer, called into full-time work, and Spirit-filled. I rested in this confidence, never actively seeking a mate.

Meanwhile, my search intensified for a Jewish believer to invite to the university, someone who could help me present Messiah's claims to the Jewish students and whoever else would attend our meetings. Later that spring of 1949, I heard good reports from a friend about a Jewish speaker and teacher in Atlanta, Georgia. My friend gave me the man's name and address, and I wrote to him, inviting him to come, agreeing to cover his transportation and other expenses, and to find him a place to stay on campus. His name was Martin Chernoff, and he accepted my invitation.

I made arrangements for Mr. Chernoff to stay with the president of InterVarsity and raised the money for his traveling expenses by selling some of my college text books. I set up speaking engagements for him with the fraternities, lined up some of my high-school friends and a few Jewish girlfriends for another special meeting, and scheduled a couple of other speaking engagements in town.

When Mr. Chernoff arrived, in June, I was surprised to find that he was a young man. For some reason, he was also surprised to find that I was only a sophomore. Somehow my letters had failed to communicate that point. I was not the "older woman" he expected to meet who was working with Jewish students.

Kurt and his radical fraternity brothers, and a few of my personal friends who came to listen, were deeply affected by all Marty had to say. Several promised to pray, asking God to show them if Jesus truly was the Messiah. The high point of the week for me was when Marty and I led my best high-school girlfriend to the Messiah.

Marty stayed one week, sharing his vision of a Jewish revival from a Biblical point of view. When he left campus, he and I had spent a lot of time together talking about the Jewish people, about our respective callings, and about the future. He secured for himself a special place in my heart and life, even though we did not speak of any such thing at the time.

Later that same month, to my great surprise, Marty wrote and asked me to marry him.

Chapter Seven

Two Become One

Can two walk together, unless they are agreed?
Amos 3:3, NKJ

1949-1953: Knoxville, Atlanta, Toronto

I stared at the letter in my hand and at the tract he had enclosed entitled, *"Be Ye Filled With the Spirit."* Amazed, I thought again about my impressions of Marty Chernoff. In our one, short week together, I had developed a tremendous liking and respect for him, but there had been no wave of romantic love. Now, suddenly, he was proposing marriage to me. I had to think about him now, not only as a friend, but as a potential husband.

I was barely nineteen, while he was almost twenty-nine. He was balding, but that just made him appear intellectual, like a "thinker," and he was handsome. He was short, three full inches shorter than my five-foot-nine-plus frame. He was quiet and unassuming, but powerful, the most spiritually dynamic man I had ever met, a man of intense prayer and deep spirituality. He was Jewish. He was called to minister to his people, and he spoke with fire. He was sold out to God - and, from the title of the little tract I held in my hand, he was also Spirit-filled. Marty filled all the requirements God had put in my heart for the man that would be my mate and more. For a week I had watched him interact with challenging, argumentative Jewish students and my friends, and he had met and embraced them all with love and respect. I liked that.

Even so, I spent much time in prayer that God would either confirm or refute Marty's conviction that we were meant for each other. Finally, early one morning, after an entire night of prayer, God confirmed His approval by giving me a specific verse of Scripture from the Psalms:

> *Thou hast led Thy people as a flock by the hand of Moses and Aaron.* Psalm 77:20

Moses and Aaron - two called to work together as one *"hand,"* to lead God's flock. As I meditated on the verse, I realized how intimately God knew my heart, how I had yearned for a united family, for a father at home, for brothers and sisters; how I longed to marry, to become one *"hand"* with my husband, to serve God's flock, and to have children of my own. I wanted to say with Ruth the Moabitess, who like me was not Jewish by birth, but by calling:

> *Do not urge me to desert you by turning away from you; because wherever you go, there I will go; wherever you lodge I will lodge. Your people are my people, and your God is my God. Wherever you die I will die, and there I shall be buried. Thus may God do to me and worse if anything but death separates you and me.* Ruth 1:16-17

As dawn broke and I waited in God's presence by my window, I was conscious of His strong leading and approval. I arose with the conviction that God had not only called me, but that he had called Marty and me together to minister to the Jewish people for the rest of our lives.

Two Become One

With this realization, a great surge of love flooded my heart for this man I hardly knew.

Our courtship was unique. We had met on June 10, 1949; his letter of proposal arrived later that same month. On August 15, I accepted, and we set our wedding date for September 5, less than three months after we had first met. Looking back, it is easy to see that it was not a normal courtship and not normally a sound thing to do, committing your life to someone without a waiting period of a year or more. But the Lord showed me then that I had already done my homework, spiritually speaking. After that powerful, life-changing experience with the Holy Spirit, I had surrendered every aspect of my life to the Lord. When God brought up the issue of marriage, I had settled it once and for all: My marriage was in His hands. Then He had laid it firmly upon my heart to marry someone Jewish, someone already committed to His Jewish people, someone already working somewhere.

After I had read Marty's letter and prayed over it a while, there was no doubt in my mind that God's "somebody for me" was Martin Chernoff, the man who fulfilled all the qualifications. And the Lord Himself gave neither of us any reason to wait.

The members of my small Nazarene Church were not pleased with this turn of events. They had already decided among themselves that God wanted me to marry a fellow member of InterVarsity Fellowship, a young man who also attended their church. Their reasons for believing that it was not God's will for me to marry Marty were the same reasons that I would have had for being skeptical of the circumstances. It was all happening much too fast. We hardly knew each other. Nothing about the match seemed to follow the lines of conventional wisdom.

Born a Jew...Die a Jew

The pastor, therefore, took a strong stand against this marriage. While I held firmly to the leading God had given me, she was so troubled that she fasted and prayed that the Lord would intervene and bring us to our senses. On the third day of her fast, however, the Lord spoke to her, instructing her to stop praying against that which He had ordained.

As she waited before Him in awe, she received a confirming vision from God: Gates of pearl swung wide open to receive a stream of worshipping Jewish people, flowing through them into the Kingdom of God. Suddenly, she gasped in remorse, as she saw Marty and me, standing side-by-side, holding open those gates. At the very next service, she repented, weeping before the congregation, making apology from behind the pulpit, and testifying to what God had shown her. The intercessors were not to oppose us. A move of God's Spirit was coming in which God was going to use Marty and me together - as one hand.

On September 5, Marty and I were married by a friend of his in Atlanta. I wore a pretty brown-crepe dress and flat-heeled shoes. Our witnesses were my wonderful, born-again Aunt Ruth, who prayed throughout the ceremony, and my mother, who cried as she watched all her dreams for her only child go up in smoke. Jewish people were strangers to her. In her world, I had become a social embarrassment.

For me, it was a mysteriously wonderful and exciting venture, crossing over into a new world. In just a little over three years, I had been born again, received a call to the Jewish people, met and come to know and love many of them, and married the Jewish man God Himself had chosen for me. Ours was an experience much like Abraham and Sarah's: Like them, we, too, left our families, our cultures and our own people for a place

Two Become One

and people largely unknown to us. Unlike them, Marty's family, culture and people had nothing in common with mine, nor mine with his.

Our concepts of money were also worlds apart. Coming from a very sheltered background, I held romanticized, idealized views of what it might mean to "walk by faith, and not by sight," but I had much to learn. Marty, on the other hand, already had some practical experience in this regard, having been diligently trying to raise support by sending out newsletters in the name of *The Gospel Harvester*.

After a wonderful week of honeymoon in beautiful Gatlinburg, Tennessee in the Smokey Mountains, Marty and I settled into our "garden apartment" on Ponce de Leon Avenue in the heart of Atlanta's Jewish district, a combination kitchen/living-room/bedroom with a pull-down bed and a private bath - in a basement. Our cozy nest would prove to be the proverbial School of Hard Knocks. Our schooling began that same day at the post office, where we went to collect the checks mailed in response to Marty's newsletter, and found nothing in our box but dust.

Marty had a dollar in his pocket, but I had nothing in mine. We had no money in the bank, no silverware, no dishes, no kitchen utensils, no pots, no pans. Someone had left us a pound of coffee, so we bought bread and peanut butter with the dollar, spread peanut butter on the bread with a toothbrush handle, and made coffee in the aluminum ice-cube tray from the refrigerator, while thanking the Lord for His provision.

Mother had packed all my winter clothes in a steamer trunk and shipped it from Knoxville to Atlanta. But even after cold weather set in, we had no money to get the trunk out of storage. Eventually, we were able to redeem it in the spring. The trunk made a nice bureau, our one-

and-only bureau. Experience was teaching us to discern the difference between faith and presumption, and to be thankful for everything we had.

One of our first lessons learned jointly came through tithing, and as we counted the few coins and bills that came into our hands, we had many opportunities to put the concepts of Malachi 3:10 into practice to "prove God":

Bring the whole tithe into the storehouse, so there may be food in My house, and by this put Me to the test, says the LORD of hosts, if I will not open the windows of heaven for you and pour out for you a more than sufficient blessing.

According to the Scriptures, God wanted the top 10 percent of our gross income. At first, this was very painful for us to obey. When we added up the cost of our absolute necessities, like food and bus fare, it always totalled more than 90 percent of what we had on hand. But God proved Himself over and again, and soon we realized that somehow, in God's economy, the 90 percent left after tithing always stretched farther than the 100 percent would have covered by itself!

After we had been "home" a few weeks, Marty showed me a letter he had received from his mother. She wrote, "It's enough now already that you are *meshumed*. Just make sure you don't marry a *shiksa* (non-Jewish woman)!"

"What did you tell her?" I asked him.

"That we were already married, that I had wanted to marry someone Jewish, but there just weren't that many Jewish believers. I searched. Then I met you, and I knew you were the one."

Marty's mother and siblings were shocked with this news. By marrying a *goy* (Gentile), they felt Marty was

Two Become One

turning his back on the God of his Fathers, on the Jewish people, and on his heritage. Years of pogroms and hatred by professed Christians prevented them from understanding the trust Marty had found in *Yeshua* as his Messiah.

Marty and I agreed that we needed to face this problem, to travel up to Toronto to visit his mother, his brothers, Jack and Smitty, and his sister Sophie, so he could introduce me to them and them to me. We could use the trip to good advantage. On our way to Toronto, while we were there, and on our way back, we could visit Canadian and American ministries to Jewish people, to see what worked for others and what did not. We wanted our labor among the Jewish people to be effectual, and the trip would offer many potentially profitable learning opportunities. How we would raise the finances for the trip remained a mystery, but we felt we should go as soon as possible. Miraculously, the Lord provided the funds through well-timed contributions.

Helen was superficially polite to me at first, and understandably troubled at her son's having married a *shiksa*. Jack and Smitty and their wives, Hilda and Sonia, accepted me graciously, but Sophie was deeply resentful and openly hostile.

Helen spoke English well enough, but she preferred Yiddish, and, at first, she and Sophie spoke only Yiddish in front of me, knowing that I could not understand any of what was being said. Finally, one day I overheard Marty say to his mother, "Mom, I love you, and I want to keep coming here, but Joanna is my wife. If you can't be nice to her, then you might not see as much of me as you would like." He made it plain that there was no turning back; she would have to accept me or lose him.

I knew this was hard for her. At the same time, I was deeply grateful to the Holy Spirit for having infused my heart with supernatural love for all Jewish people, and I marveled that it worked so well under these circumstances. So much godly patience and love for my Jewish family was working in my spirit, that no amount of rejection from them could touch me. Even though I was just a young girl of nineteen, my special love from God for my mother-in-law made it hard for her to resist and stand against me for long. I made a conscious effort to win her favor. Knowing that she kept a strict kosher kitchen, I asked her to instruct me in *kashrut* (rules for keeping kosher). Eventually she agreed.

Kosher, I discovered, means *"fit, proper, appropriate, permissible."* Under kosher guidelines, all meat - and only meat from specified animals - must be slaughtered by a religious slaughterer, who inspects it for disease, impurities and abnormalities. It must be properly killed and bled, the sciatic nerve removed, then stamped by a supervisor.

Meat and milk products are not to be eaten at the same meal or sooner than six hours apart. Separate utensils for meat and dairy are used. Every kosher kitchen must have two sets of dishes, silverware, pots and pans, dish cloths and towels, even separate refrigerators.

Because eating and drinking are acts of worship for Orthodox Jews, special prayers are always said before and after meals. During cleanup after one meal, I made a *kashrut* mistake with a table knife. To make it kosher again I had to take it outdoors, bury it in the ground, dig it up, and bring it back inside.

During our times together, Helen also taught me some rudimentary Yiddish words and phrases:

Ich liebe dich. "I love you."
Zie-shtil! "Keep quiet!"
Gay shluffen. "Go to sleep."
And many others.

Two Become One

I came to love her dearly, and felt deep compassion for her in her widowhood. Smitty, Hilda and their baby Susan lived upstairs. From their many examples of kindnesses to "Ma," and me, I learned much about Jewish family care and love.

While we were in Toronto, Marty and I also visited the Nathaniel Institute where he had come to know the Lord. The Kays were thrilled to see Marty again and to meet me. As always, they were warm and full of love, taking time with us, and showing a deep personal interest in our affairs. They were such loving people and had experienced such success in sharing the Messiah with Jewish people, that they became role models for us.

God was laying an important stone into the foundation of our ministry. He was the Chief Cornerstone, but He used the Kays to set the foundation stone of love as expressed in warm, welcoming hospitality and personal interest.

We also visited the Bruneaus at Covenant House, where Marty had discovered the writings of Charles Finney, and learned much about repentance and prevailing prayer in the spirit. During our visits there, God set two other foundation stones for us, those of intercessory prayer, and of the supernatural gifts, fruit, and power of the Holy Spirit.

In Atlanta, we met Cam Thompson, president of the Pan American Testament League, a mighty prayer warrior who literally ran his ministry from his knees in his prayer chamber. Through Cam, God reinforced our faith in persevering, intercessory prayer - for all our personal needs, for others, for our ministry, and even for our unborn children.

Unexpectedly, some of the answers we were seeking came indirectly, but loud and clear through some ministries' negative approaches and attitudes. For example, the first valuable negative conclusion I drew was that intellectual debate is not God's pathway to success!

Marty already knew this. From Earl Bruneau's teaching, Marty had already decided to lay aside his expository books. But now, sadly, we were seeing and hearing many workers in the field laboring hard at debate with learned rabbis and Hebrew scholars, presenting compellingly brilliant arguments with Jewish people in their shops and in their homes, propounding *"the letter"* of *"the Law,"* but the spirit of love was missing, and there was, consequently, nothing that *"makes alive"* and brings results (2 Corinthians 3:6). We saw that when they won the argument they usually lost the person. We came away warned that God did not want us to go the way of intellectual debate.

At other places we visited, we learned to beware of unbelief. An *"evil heart of unbelief"* (Hebrews 3:12, NKJ) was undermining the very thing some of the workers were trying to accomplish. They simply did not believe that God was going to save many Jewish people. Often, they would labor for a year, or even two or more years, before they saw a single Jewish person come to faith in the Messiah as a result of their efforts. They thought even that was wonderful. "God does not expect us to look for results," they often said to one another. "We just sow the seed, then leave the results to Him." Because of that attitude, many new professions of faith proved weak and, therefore, short-lived.

Other workers taught new believers to expect their families to divorce them, to ban them from fellowship, to recite *kaddish* over them. According to them, it was still the right thing to do to accept *Yeshua* as the Messiah, then become assimilated into a denominational church. New believers, they said, should pull away from their families, from all unbelievers, and join themselves

Two Become One

to the Christians. "Your family will desert you," they would say, "but that is the price you must pay here on earth for eternal life in the hereafter."

What kind of Good News is that? we asked ourselves. No wonder it was so painfully hard for Jewish people to accept the Lord in those years. When one member in a family got saved, he tended to be the only one. The families that recited *kaddish* found symbolic death of the family member vastly more acceptable to the clan than the treachery of identifying with those whose "Christianity" led to slaughtering Jews. No wonder morale among those workers was so low! As Marty and I studied the Word together, we began to feel that God's will was just the opposite, and to see so many Jewish families torn apart because of religious differences must surely break His heart.

With all of this, visiting Toronto was, for me, a pure delight. During our six-week stay, I often wandered out into the streets of the immigrant section to browse the shops and stalls, listening to the strange accents, watching the people, and trying to feel what it was like to be Jewish. In my heart, I was trying to absorb and sort through all these new experiences and new concepts. Having been exposed to the mainly homogeneous cities of the southeastern United States, I found the anomalous immigrant districts of Toronto exciting and moving. I felt I was getting to know the heart of the Jewish people.

By the middle of March, when we returned home from our trip, I was five months pregnant. Marty, who had always cultivated his natural affinity with children, was thrilled.

We realized that God was also building the walls to our ministry, and we reviewed what we had learned so far: The chief substance was love. Intellectual debate was not for us. Unbelief was to be rooted out and rejected. Family salvation was a principle clearly found in God's Word. The Holy Spirit was to be our only source of power. We fully believed that prevailing prayer would bring God's will to fruition.

We had learned to pray, to pray without ceasing, to pray nights, to pray days, to fast and to pray - and to tithe and pray. From every dollar that came into the ministry, we had already learned to give God the first dime. God was faithful and blessed our giving, but there were many times of dire stress about money that were hard on both of us, the only truly unresolved dissension throughout our entire marriage.

Marty was very "Old World" about money, keeping it all to himself, and doling it out to me for whatever I said we needed, when he had it. He never told me how much we had. He had assumed responsibility for supporting us, and he did not want me to worry about money. He never understood that it did not work that way with me, especially when bills were due or overdue. I even tried baby-sitting to bring in a little extra cash, but it paid so little, and emotionally it was not worth it. Wealthy believers often assured us they were praying for all our needs to be met, when often what we needed was a loaf of bread.

Regardless, we always tithed, and God continued to supply our necessities, though seldom more, and in time, giving to others out of our deep personal need became not only a challenge, but our deep personal joy.

Gradually, we began to see and recognize God's specific answers to our own specific prayers for daily provisions, for food, rent, clothing, bus fare, and eventually (after two years) a car. Like pioneers of old, however, our life was hard. Money was scarce, and true friends and lovers of Israel were few.

Two Become One

Nevertheless, our joy abounded on August 20, 1950, when Joel Martin was born, and again when David Lee followed thirteen months later, on October 3, 1951, not long after Marty gained his American citizenship.

It was during this blessed time in our lives together, that Marty first shared with me the stunning vision he had received from the Lord in 1948 before we were married: A mighty revival among the young Jewish people, like the harvest of a vast orchard of trees and vines laden with ripened fruit, encompassing the United States, even the world - the first of his three major visions that would affect and shape the rest of his life.

One day, when Marty entered into deep intercession for just such a revival to come to pass even in his lifetime, the Lord graciously rewarded him with a thrilling confirmation through a direct word from the Scriptures, straight from the heart of God into Marty's soul:

> *Ask from the Lord rain in the time of the latter rain.*
> *... He will give you rain in abundance.*
>
> Zechariah 10:1

> *He will cause the rain to come down for you - the former rain, and the latter rain ... before the coming of the great and terrible day of the Lord.*
>
> Joel 2:23, 31, NKJ

Greatly moved, Marty shared the revelation from God with me, and together we were awed that Almighty God would speak to us in this way.

Shortly thereafter, my Aunt Ruth, who loved us and loved baby-sitting our boys, sold her home and bought a larger house, which she then had renovated into a duplex. She lived in one side, and we lived in the other.

Her generous arrangement provided ample shelter for us and our growing family. The large, pleasant living room was ideal for holding Bible studies.

In 1951, someone gave us a car, a 1932 Ford. We drove it for two years, often chauffeuring those who did not live near city transportation lines to our home for Bible study, then back home again. Since the car was already almost twenty years old, we could never find parts for it and finally were forced to abandon it. During that time, however, it was a great blessing. By visiting survivors of the Holocaust, we had learned to appreciate what we had. We needed that, because the next few years of this pioneering work would prove to be very difficult. We would need God's love and grace to deal with the challenges we would soon face.

PART II

CHAPTER EIGHT

CLASHES WITH THE ESTABLISHMENT CHURCH

For Zion's sake I will not keep silent, and for Jerusalem's sake I will not rest, until her righteousness shines forth brightly and her salvation radiates as a lamp.   Isaiah 62:1

1953-1960: ATLANTA, CINCINNATI

To both of us, love meant family, and we continually prayed over our two boys that God's perfect plan for them would be realized in their lives. We talked to them continually about the importance of having their sins forgiven and having *Yeshua* living in their hearts.

Marty was a wonderful, loving disciplinarian, making sure we had the boys' attention, playing with them, training them at all times, not just when they misbehaved.

We continued to be greatly distressed over the dissolution of Jewish families when one member of the family got saved and joined one of the mainstream churches. Many of our Jewish relatives and friends asked us, "Are you going to become like those people who have been persecuting us for two thousand years?"

We subscribed to the *Herald of His Coming,* a deeply spiritual, monthly magazine that fed and sustained us throughout our entire ministry. It was published by believers in California who spent much of their time on their knees praying for revival in America. Almost all the *Herald* articles emphasized at least one of three specific doctrines: 1) that the Holy Spirit was at work in revival power in the world today; 2) that Bible prophecy paralleled current events; and 3) that God specialized in families and planned for the entire family to be saved, not just one member.

These strong teachings reinforced the concepts that God was already revealing to us about love and family from every part of the Bible. As we worked these three doctrines in among our ministry foundation stones of love, the Holy Spirit, prayer and believing faith, we became firmly convinced that our entire ministry was to be focused on family-salvation principles - a totally radical concept in ministry to the Jewish people at that time.

We began to act on what we believed. When a Jewish person we knew came to the Lord, we first led that person lovingly through the preliminary steps to repentance, then taught, trained and discipled him or her to get deep into the Word, to be immersed in water and then in the Holy Spirit, to show love and concern to their families, and to turn immediately to believing prayer for family and loved ones.

"Believe God for His best," we said. "Your husband, your wife, your children, your mother, your father, your grandparents, your friends are all going to become believers in the Messiah. Show them love. Show them concern. Pray, and keep on praying." God led us to work with each believer one-on-one, and to pray for the salvation of the entire family.

As we attended to the needs of other families, God blessed our own. We watched our two beautiful boys growing straight and strong physically, and in the nurture and admonition of the Lord.

Clashes With the Establishment Church

Meanwhile, we visited several churches in and around Atlanta, but never found one where we truly felt at home. We attended Pentecostal churches, where we heard about the Spirit-filled life, with speaking in tongues, supernatural faith, and healing. At that time, however, we saw none of the other six supernatural gifts manifested in those particular churches, no *"message[s] of wisdom," "utterance[s] of knowledge," "miraculous powers," "prophecy," "discrimination between spirits,"* or *"the ability to interpret tongues"* (1 Corinthians 12:8-10).

Atlanta itself was a strong Southern Baptist bastion. Even though Marty spoke in a few Baptist churches, about anti-Semitism and the Holocaust in general, and about the need to reach all Jewish people with the Good News of the Messiah in particular, few responded positively to our ministry. Very few believers at that time were ready to financially support an independent ministry to God's Chosen People. This was, in part, because of four separate cases of fraudulence that had been perpetrated by people claiming to be reaching out to the Jewish people in the Atlanta area. Consequently, we suffered from the resulting suspicions that all people in ministry to the Jewish people were thieves.

By the end of 1953, it was obvious that all our streams of support in Atlanta had dried up. We took this as a sign that God was moving us out, but to where? Our widowed mothers lived far apart: one in Toronto, the other in Knoxville. We both felt somewhat responsible for their welfare and took that into consideration while praying about where we should move.

We spread out our map and began to pray, "Lord, where?" Soon, our attention jointly centered on Cincinnati, Ohio, the "Queen City of the West," located on the north shore of the Ohio River. When we realized that Cincinnati was situated approximately halfway between

Born a Jew...Die a Jew

Toronto and Knoxville, that helped us to make our decision. When we heard, through the "Hebrew Christian Alliance of America" grapevine, about Jewish believers living in Cincinnati, we took that as confirmation that Cincinnati was God's open door to us.

In 1954, we said good-bye to Atlanta and to Aunt Ruth, and moved "by faith" to Cincinnati. We lived temporarily in a Salvation Army camp dormitory until we found a two-bedroom apartment near the Jewish district. Right away, we met the Adlers, a Jewish family that believed in *Yeshua,* and immediately we started midweek Bible studies in their home for the few Jewish and non-Jewish believers they knew. Some of them brought their unsaved friends to the meetings to study with us. In that nonthreatening home environment, they could ask questions freely, and many heard the Good News of the Messiah there for the first time.

As a group, we visited several denominational churches in the area, but soon agreed that the deeper we dug into the *Brit Hadashah,* the hungrier we became for the full manifestation of the Holy Spirit in our midst. In our home meetings, we emphasized prayer for entire families, and God blessed. All the Adlers accepted the Messiah as their Savior: their five children, and his mother and father. Before long three generations of Adlers were worshipping together. Because thorough discipling takes time, we spent much time with these precious new believers.

Then, out of the blue, Al Adler, for some reason known only to him, turned back to the world and became very hostile toward his wife and her profession as a believer. When Ruth came to us brokenhearted, we reminded her, first of all, that her husband absolutely could be reclaimed. The Bible said, that because of the sanctified wife, the husband was set aside for the Lord (1

Clashes With the Establishment Church

Corinthians 7:14). We would pray, believing that specific scriptural promise for Al.

Al became verbally abusive, but instead of becoming upset with him, Ruth became sweeter and more compliant. Whatever menial things he demanded of her, she would do without murmuring or complaining, *"as unto the Lord."* Finally, one night, at an all-night prayer meeting, where Ruth had come to pray for her husband, we heard a loud crash. In came Al, running. He flung himself down, repenting with tears, and begged her forgiveness.

Joyfully, she forgave him. They were quickly reconciled, their marriage stronger than ever. She told us later that if Marty and I had not both pressed her diligently to pray for Al, they might have ended up in divorce court. The four of us soon became close and intimate friends, with Al being one of Marty's most compatible prayer partners.

Our apartment complex was loud and rowdy, with unruly neighborhood children sometimes battling each other with sticks, metal garbage-can lids and stones. Remembering the little 5-year-old boy who had been so impacted with the Gospel back in Knoxville, I decided to teach a series of four children's Bible study classes. Our own boys could benefit, and we hoped to pull in some of the neighborhood children, as well. It worked. We witnessed great changes in many of them.

Meanwhile, as I observed the older children outside on the playground, I came to recognize and appreciate the contrasting results between parochial and public-school education. The Catholic-school students were mostly attentive, listening and responding politely when spoken to, while many of the others seemed to lack these desired traits. Marty and I soon became staunch advocates of religious training, and made it a priority to keep our children always in religious schools.

The majority of the Jewish people in Cincinnati were financially either middle or upper-middle class at that time. Although we were strained financially during those years, from 1959 to 1970, I felt that, in order to witness to the Jewish people, we needed to live among them and to maintain a standard of living to approximate theirs.

I wanted to keep our house neat and clean and well maintained, and to have nice clothes and nourishing food for our boys. Marty wanted those things too, but, whether we were working with an organization or independently, he tended to trust the Lord to determine our standard of living more than I did. It bothered me that sometimes our sons went to school with holes in their pants and that the other children had lunch boxes with special treats, while ours had brown bags with often scanty rations. Sometimes things were better; but sometimes they were worse. Our house, however, was always a haven of love, where we stressed the importance of family and relationships.

Despite our differences over the scarcity of money and the handling of it, we somehow learned to love and respect each other and to continue serving the Lord. Then, early in 1955, when we received an offer to become full-time, salaried laborers with an organization that ministered among Jewish people, we jumped at it. Money for the salaries of those who served in the organization came mainly from evangelical Christian supporters, as it was associated with a large and well-known Bible college. This was understandable. There was no such thing as Messianic Judaism or Messianic synagogues. There were not many Jewish believers in *Yeshua* in the United States or anywhere else in the world for that matter. So the ministry to the Jewish people, by necessity, was an out-

Clashes With the Establishment Church

growth of the Gentile Christian church establishment, and all support for Jewish believers and their ministries, at that time, came primarily from the church.

Since then we have learned that while we should always welcome support from Gentile believers, independent Messianic Judaism is preferable because of the freedom it gives us to be as Jewish as the Lord leads us. Anti-Semitism within the established church has often hindered the work of the Lord among His People, and we find that we can be a clearer light for the Messiah *Yeshua*, to our own people, by having our own houses of worship. At the time, however, this was just not possible. It was not yet God's time for Messianic Judaism to reappear on the world scene.

The church-establishment mentality of the organization we were now working for was firmly entrenched; therefore their prescribed immediate first step for Jews who became believers was to be brought under the spiritual oversight of a mainline, evangelical church. Since there were no visible alternatives - no other place for them to go, and no other source of support for the workers - we had no choice but to go along; but this situation caused us a great deal of concern. Somehow we discerned a great gap between "converting" our Jewish people to Christianity, which inherently split up their families, and proclaiming to them the Good News that *Yeshua* is the Jewish Messiah.

Following methods of evangelism established during an earlier era of increased Jewish immigration (at the turn of the century), leaders of the organization believed that the one and only way to share the Good News of the Messiah with Jewish people was to pass out New Testaments and tracts door-to-door and store-to-store. They had been doing it that way for fifty years, ever since they first distributed Gospel tracts among Jewish immigrants coming off the boats. The method had shown a degree of success back then, so why change?

So, the day that we received our letter of acceptance as workers of the organization, we also received tracts and New Testaments, and work sheets that we were to fill out and return each month, reporting to headquarters exactly how many Testaments we had passed out that month, how many tracts we had distributed, how many visitations we had made, how much money we had taken in, and any other details we could provide about what we had done for the ministry.

For two specific reasons, we did not follow the mission's guidelines of going door-to-door and store-to-store. (1) Someone much like the infamous Jack-the-Ripper was terrifying the neighborhoods in Cincinnati. We could not, therefore, get a foot in anyone's door. People were too frightened to open their doors to strangers. (2) We did not have the heart for it. We strongly believed God had called us to a personal, "family-contact-leads ministry," a more pastoral ministry, encourage those to whom we ministered to witness to their own immediate families, to socialize with their families and friends, to love them and to help them. That is what we were already doing full-time, and we continued as we had throughout the late 50s, being very content with the method, because we saw success - Jewish people coming to faith in the Savior. So we conducted weekly meetings in our home with primarily Jewish believers. In these meetings we ministered to their personal needs, taught them the Bible, led them in prayer, and encouraged them to show God's love to their non-believing family members. These informal, small groups soon took on a distinctively Jewish flavor.

For us, it was wonderful time, nothing at all like the early years of our marriage, when we were out there

Clashes With the Establishment Church

alone, getting cold shoulders and closed doors, little response from speaking in churches, and even less from our newsletters. We were also very thankful to be getting a check every month, very happy to have a supportive spiritual family - the organizational board - behind us.

One day the Lord spoke to my heart:

Say to your brother, "My people, " and to your sister, "Beloved. "... See! I shall allure her [Israel]; I will take her to the wilderness, I will speak tenderly to her heart.

Hosea 2:1, 14

We were learning, by doing, what it meant to be one with our people.

As a family, we did everything together, including opening our home to ministers and travelers from other nations, making our home a place where something was always happening. Since our boys were growing up fast, I also made our home the welcome-center for the neighborhood children. When other parents sent their kids out to play, I tried to see that they all ended up in our yard. Then we did fun things together, trying to make their life enjoyable, and trying to have some spiritual excitement from which everyone could benefit, as they learned that serving *Yeshua* could be fun.

In August 1955, for the first time, we took our boys and our small home group of Jewish and non-Jewish believers to Indiana for a week-long "Prophecy and the Jew" conference convened by the organization. Most of the conference leaders were either Bible college professors or, at least, Bible scholars. They each taught wonderfully exciting lessons from both Old and New Testaments, paralleling Bible prophecy with current events. When there was time, the field-evangelists would take turns speaking about their own work in the field. We returned home to Cincinnati strengthened and encouraged by having fellowshipped with other workers and from having heard other Jewish believers tell how they came to believe in *Yeshua* as their Messiah. Some of the older conferees had been coming year after year, some for as long as twenty or thirty years.

After that, Marty and I attended every year. The third time we went, in 1957, we took our entire group along, and our three children (two-month-old Hope Sharon had been born in June following my three miscarriages since the birth of David).

Hope was truly a miracle child. When the enemy tried to steal her from us in midterm, I went forward in a service for prayer for her healing, and God heard our plea, giving us the supernatural gift of faith - literally the *"substance of things hoped for, the evidence of things not [yet] seen"* (Hebrews 11:1, NKJ). Despite all the symptoms to the contrary, I knew that I was healed and that this child would be full-term. In fact, I was so sure that, back at our new house, I loaded my arms with heavy boxes and literally ran up the stairs with them, praising God that I was healed. The next morning all the symptoms of miscarriage were gone and, in the fullness of time, Hope Sharon made her squalling entrance to the world, accompanied by sounds of great celebration on our part.

As a growing group of Jewish believers in *Yeshua,* we knew we needed to be established in a place of worship where we could mature in the Spirit-filled life. Discerning that we were called by God to be in some way "different," we began searching for a special place where we would all be accepted and comfortable. We visited and explored many local churches in and around Cincinnati, looking for the place where we would truly feel at home. Although we praised God for the wonderful

Clashes With the Establishment Church

support of those Gentile believers who loved the Jewish people, we still felt like outsiders.

We visited one little Bible church which honored the Word of God and welcomed Jewish people, but refused to recognize two things that were vital to us: that the total immersion in the Holy Spirit was valid for today, and that our own ministry to Jewish people was valid.

At a "deliverance tabernacle," we witnessed some spectacular healings and found true commitment to prayer for End-Time Revival, but when we realized that these people had gone off into deep error, we got out quickly and tried a large, conservative Baptist church, where we had enrolled our boys in day school. We continued searching the Scriptures and teaching our group at home about the power of God and gifts of the Holy Spirit.

We studied on the periphery and taught on this for about three or four years, while God exercised both of us about our own need to be filled with the Spirit. Finally, in June 1960, at a church Marty and I were attending, we both received a renewed infilling of the Holy Spirit, this time with our own manifestations of prophecy and tongues. Marty also received a personal prophecy: that he had received the gift of healings. At this time, in prayer, the Lord showed Marty that if he resigned from the organization he was working with, God would make him more fruitful in the ministry, and he could move in the fullness of the Spirit. High in the spirit, we went home and immediately introduced joyful, Spirit-filled praise and worship, with hand-clapping, into our little home group.

We now faced a dilemma. The tightly organized, very conservative Baptist church the whole group was attending had something planned for the members of our Bible study group almost every night from Sunday through

Born a Jew...Die a Jew

Friday: Monday night, visitation; Wednesday night, family-night; Thursday night, something else; Friday night, who-knows-what. As a result, the Jewish believers stopped showing up at our midweek Bible studies designed specifically for Jewish people to learn about *Yeshua* as their Messiah, and to fellowship together as Jewish believers.

At the church, the newly saved Jewish believers faced two conflicting waves: On the one hand, as the church's "token Jews," they were made to feel guilty about "backsliding" if they were not attending all the planned meetings; on the other hand, they were being patted on the back and flattered by such inappropriate and ingratiating compliments as, "Oh, you're so wonderful! A saved Jew! Come, be our usher," or, "Here's a Sunday school class you can teach." While they were prematurely pressured to become leaders in the congregation, understandably some of the older members resented them. We had even heard such comments as, "The Jews are taking over the church!" But, even more devastating to our way of thinking, while becoming not-so-subtly "assimilated," they were rapidly losing their burden for their own people's salvation. They were beginning to assimilate and be lost to their Jewish people forever.

In 1960, the Baptist pastor let words slip out of his mouth that indicated his deep-rooted prejudice against Jewish people. We tried to forgive and forget, but his words hurt us deeply, and we found ourselves once again withdrawing emotionally from the organized church. Later, we recognized that God's hand was in this, to move us in new directions.

Finding comfort and great enjoyment from playing the piano, I began composing original words honoring the Messiah *Yeshua* and putting them to old Yiddish melodies. One composition was, *"He Put Laughter into*

Clashes With the Establishment Church

My Soul," set to the tune of the old Yiddish wedding song, *Ich vill zich speilen* ("I want to dance"):

O come, let's sing - let us rejoice.
O come, let's sing - let us rejoice.
Messiah's come - and He's brought joy.
O, He's brought laughter into my soul.

I once was dead - my spirit cold.
I had no joy - far from the fold.
Messiah came - He made me sing.
O, He's brought laughter into my soul.

To the best of my knowledge, then and now, there was no other such music available at that time. This proved to be a key step in the development of our ministry, toward the Messianic movement we would be instrumental in establishing.

When the church we were attending suffered a disheartening split, our own group had grown to between fifty and sixty regular members. Some of our men came to Marty and said, "We're tired of going back and forth between denominational churches. We're always uncomfortable, never knowing how they truly feel about us. Why can't we have our own congregation?"

Al Adler quickly spoke up. "We can!" he said. "Ruth and I have a big house. Instead of crowding into the Chernoff's living room, we can meet in our recreation room."

We all agreed. Marty and I would still remain salaried by the organization, sending any and all monies collected to them, but we would also have our own congregation, celebrating the Lord according to the way we understood the Bible.

Born a Jew...Die a Jew

It was a pragmatic decision, not because we had a vision of any clearly defined "new thing" God was doing, but from necessity. We saw Jewish believers spiritually blossoming best among their own people and under our teaching. Even though we still sang wonderful, old, traditional hymns from the hymn books, and still visited denominational churches from time to time on Sunday nights, we were "charismatic Hebrew-Christians," radicals in the Body of believers.

Soon, we began unofficially calling ourselves the "Hebrew-Christian Baptist Congregation," still deeply entrenched in the Christian church, still part of the Hebrew-Christian movement, and still associating ourselves with Christian culture. What a long way we had to go! I look back now on that period, shocked at how foreign it all seems.

Since the members of the organization we were still associated with generally rejected immersion in the Holy Spirit as a separate experience from that of salvation, we felt that we should leave them, though we loved them all. Marty felt constrained to discuss our situation with the born-again Jewish President of the group. He felt honor bound to tell the man about our immersion in the *Ruach HaKodesh* (Holy Spirit) and our call to pray over the sick.

The president was not against our profession of the work of the Holy Spirit in our lives as much as he was against our fledgling congregation's meeting in the Adlers' home. "Our organization is not in the habit of starting Jewish congregations," he said. "We don't like it, but you should not resign. Stay with us. You don't have to preach about the Holy Spirit, do you? We'll overlook it. We want you to stay, but we also want you to disband your so-called congregation. Remember that

Clashes With the Establishment Church

you are an evangelist, not a pastor or a congregation planter, yes?"

We talked it over among ourselves, but soon realized that encouraging our group to draw their families and friends into our circle was but one of many areas where we continually clashed with the organizational board. Mainly, we felt that pastoring our people, including the new believers, was a stone the Lord had quietly laid in the foundation of our ministry, and it was one area we could not now surrender.

We resigned from the organization in August 1960; and, from that moment, to our profound dismay, were, once again, plunged into deep financial straits. To complicate matters, Marty became very ill with emphysema, complicated by an onslaught of excruciating gout. In light of the prophecies concerning his healing ministry, I have never understood completely why he suffered in either sense. The combined attack, physical and financial, took us totally by surprise.

A robust athlete by the age seventeen, Marty had always been a strong, husky man of the outdoors. Now he suffered recurring bouts of sickness over the next several years. Once, when he was so serious that he was hospitalized, his doctor used long needles to draw the fluid out of his joints, a painful process.

Marty's bouts of sickness complicated our financial situation, for we had no medical insurance. We had stepped out on what we called "faith," but money was not coming to us like we had read about in the testimonies of great men of faith like Hudson Taylor, George Mueller, Rees Howells, and, of course, Charles Finney. This was difficult for us to understand since Marty was a strong prayer warrior and a man of great faith.

I wanted to do something, anything to help out. Since Marty was always home, and practically bedridden, I left the boys, who were eleven and twelve at the time, and little Hope, who was four, in Marty's care, and took a secretarial job. Unfortunately, my job did not bring in much money, and we nearly lost our home.

Chapter Nine

The Second Vision

Thou shalt arise, and have mercy on Zion: for the time to favour her, yea, the set time, is come.
                              Psalm 102:13 KJV

1961-1966: Cincinnati

Through all our trials, we had to keep our eyes on the Lord, and our hearts set on the promised revival. During that time, we were partly supported through our prayer newsletter, partly through offerings from speaking engagements, partly by friends and partly by our home congregation. God was blessing our family.

One night, after a meeting, our little Hope, who was four, came in singing and skipping, and when Marty asked her why she was so happy, she said, "Something happened! Something happened to me! *Yeshua* came right under my skin." How I rejoiced as the Scripture came to mind, *"Nothing affords me more joy than to hear that my children are leading the true life"* (3 John 4). But all was not well.

We had been caring for my mother in our home for several years, when suddenly, in 1961, her condition deteriorated rapidly. We rushed her to the hospital, but the doctors could not pinpoint the problem. She had not been eating properly, and was so debilitated, that the attack, something like the Asian flu, killed her. I agreed to an autopsy, and they found that she had severely dis-

Born a Jew...Die a Jew

eased kidneys - chronic pyelonephritis - a condition not easily diagnosed until the 50s. The combination of symptoms she had been exhibiting all her life, weakness and chronic exhaustion, was something she had passed on to me. How deeply I repented for unfairly labeling her a hypochondriac, for symptoms even the doctors could not precisely diagnose!

Just before Mother's funeral, I rejoiced to learn indirectly from her night nurse that all the prayers, all our witnessing by word and example, all the seeds of salvation planted into her spirit, had ultimately borne fruit. According to the nurse, a few days before Mother passed away into eternity, she had accepted the Lord's forgiveness and salvation on her death bed.

Soon thereafter, Marty's beloved mother, Helen Chernoff, also passed away. We felt greatly bereaved by our double loss, but were comforted knowing that Marty had spent time with his mother and that she too accepted the Messiah *Yeshua* just days before she went on into eternity. Someday we'll see them both again.

At some time during 1962, while listening to the radio, I heard for the first time the very popular singer, Connie Frances, sing *"My Yiddish Mama."* The song went straight to my heart, and I fell in love with Yiddish music, understanding somehow that it was important for me to bring it home to my family. I felt compelled to buy her album, and as many other Yiddish and Israeli records as I could find. From then on, I sat for hours at a time by my phonograph, playing the songs over and over, weeping, as the words and the music melded into my heart.

I also bought all the albums and music books I could find with Yiddish-European music, and played the songs night and day on the phonograph and on the piano. It was not just for my own benefit. I hoped that the haunt-

The Second Vision

ing, stirring melodies would take root also in the hearts of my children. I longed to plant a strong Jewish identity into them, so that they would identify automatically with Jewish people, even as God, through the Spirit, was making me more Jewish and giving me a love for Jewish people and their culture.

Hebrew Christians, or Jewish believers in *Yeshua* as we were called then, were taught that they were, first of all, Christians who happened to be also Jews. Our new approach, on the other hand, was leaning towards establishing our children's strong Jewish identity on the basis of their faith in *Yeshua* as the Jewish Messiah. They were Jewish people who were also believers in the Messiah.

The majority of Jewish people in Cincinnati, the hub of Reform Judaism, were descendants of German Jews, notably more assimilated into the local culture than other groups and, consequently, less interested in preserving the beloved old Yiddish melodies. As a result, remnants of Old World Jewish culture and music were fast fading from all over the city.

I felt an urgency at home to write even more original words and poems to much of the Eastern-European Yiddish music I had recently discovered, both plaintive and jubilant, eventually filling up a fifty-page song book with them. At our home-group meetings, we soon began singing only those special Jewish songs about the Lord instead of the old, traditional church hymns. This was a dynamic and important move forward in the return to our Jewish roots and identity, though we were not conscious of it at the time.

All during the period between late August 1960 and early 1963, Marty was incapacitated, off and on, with emphysema, which rendered him unable to go out, even occasionally, to speak. As sick as he was, however, we felt we could not afford for him to see a doctor on a regular basis. Besides, he argued, he believed in supernatural healing. And he did believe!

At about that time, Johnny, the brother of Joan, a member of our congregation, was severely injured in a dreadful automobile accident. His girlfriend who was with him had been killed. Johnny remained in a deep coma, while doctors and nurses urged the family to pull the plug on his life support system. They said, "It would be better for him to die than to remain as he is, with total, irreversible brain damage."

But Johnny's mother refused to give up hope. She sat with her son in his hospital room, playing tapes about the Lord, and talking to him as though he could hear her. Marty went two or three times a week to the hospital to pray for Johnny. For ten weeks, there was no response. Then one day, after Marty said, "G'bye, Johnny, see you next time," he thought he saw Johnny's fingers move.

By the time he arrived back home, his mother had called from the hospital with astonishing news. Johnny was up, awake and, except for a slight slur in his speech, perfectly healed. He had been laughing and crying, talking, and even walking up and down the halls. And no one could get him to stop! This was one of the most astonishing miracles we had ever witnessed. From all indications, Johnny should have died or remained a vegetable the rest of his life. His healing was literally a life from the dead.

As Marty continually ministered in the gifts of the Holy Spirit, with discernment of spirits, we saw miraculous healings from cancer and many other debilitating sicknesses. Although Marty himself was sick, he could lay hands on others, pray, and see them healed. No one

The Second Vision

could explain why he could not seem to get the healing he needed so much.

In late 1962, I realized that Marty was too sick with emphysema that I had to get help, whether we could afford it or not, so I took him to the hospital Emergency Unit, where he was admitted immediately.

The admitting physician was not happy with me. He said, "If you had waited another week or two, it would have been too late. Your husband would have been dead."

I called on our people and other friends and acquaintances to pray for Marty's healing. He was soon home, but still very weak, and months passed with no apparent change in his condition.

Then one day in the early spring of 1963, a week before Marty was scheduled to go back to the hospital for more treatment, an acquaintance of ours, a woman who believed that God would heal Marty, came to the house. She prayed for him, as many had done before her. We thanked her, even though Marty felt no change, and she left.

The next morning, Marty came downstairs with a strange expression on his face, and I sensed that something wonderful had happened. He confessed to me that, soon after the woman had prayed and left, the Lord had shown him what it was that hindered the healing of his present infirmity - unrecognized self-pity. He had subconsciously been feeling sorry for himself for having to suffer emphysema although he had not smoked since he tried it as a child. He repented for having allowed such a destructive attitude to take root, and asked the Lord for forgiveness and a complete cleansing. Now, the very next morning, as soon as he got up he knew that he had been completely healed!

I was skeptical. He still looked very thin and wane to me. That afternoon, however, after shooting baskets with our boys out in the open air, without becoming short of breath, Marty said to me once again, "I'm healed!"

Still unconvinced, I watched him closely. When his next head cold ran its normal course without bringing on deep chest distress, I relaxed. He had indeed been miraculously healed of emphysema, which the doctors had pronounced incurable. Now they could not find any signs that he had ever had it! Gloriously, he had experienced one of God's healing miracles for himself.

Shortly thereafter, the board for which we had worked some years wanted to rehire us, acknowledging by their offer that they considered us effective workers. But we were not so sure about returning to work with them. What did God want? Which was more important in His eyes, for us to spend our time and energy grubbing for money to survive and feed our three children? Or to accept a small salary from an organization and concentrate on the work He had called us to?

Marty seemed to have faith for everything but fundraising. He had faith for souls to be saved and discipled, and he had a strong intercessory prayer ministry. But when it came to raising money, he didn't seem to have the same optimism. I was in favor of taking the salary, and he agreed.

In June of 1963, when we returned to work with the board, it was understood that Marty was eventually expected to go out often to speak in churches as their representative, but he was under no real pressure to do so right away. What a relief to see that first pay check!

As before, there were many things that we did not agree with. We believed, for instance, that most of the ministries to Jewish people spent far too much money putting workers in the field who operated from a nega-

The Second Vision

tive point of view, having the attitude that only a few Jewish people would ever find their Messiah. Consequently, these workers became satisfied with the handful of Jewish people who became believers.

They would then direct these new Jewish believers into an existing church and forget about them. We could not let go of our new believers so easily. We felt that Jewish people who had just accepted the Messiah needed special help to grow in the Lord and to deal with their problems as Jewish followers of *Yeshua.* So, we continued meeting in the Adlers' home and, later, in our own. We took our entire group up to Indiana every summer for the "Prophecy and the Jew" conferences, and to fellowship with our old friends.

On the evening of November 22, 1963, as our country reeled from the shock of the assassination of President John F. Kennedy, Marty assembled our group together to intercede for the nation. Many of us got on our knees before the Lord, and we took turns praying aloud. Marty, however, was not praying and soon began to describe to us, with deep emotion and precise detail, what God was showing him in the spirit. This was his second great vision, a progression from the one God had given him in 1948, thirteen years earlier.

Instead of an endless orchard, signifying thousands of Jewish people *"ripe for the harvest, "* this time the vision expanded into a vast panorama. Not only multitude upon multitude of joyful Jewish people singing and laughing, and streaming into God's Kingdom from every direction, but, to Marty's utter amazement, they were young, and they were shabby. They were unkempt, all dressed in rags.

As we puzzled over this second dramatic vision, Marty heard the Lord say: **"These are My ragged, righteous remnant."**

Born a Jew...Die a Jew

Silent and motionless, we knelt in the awesome presence of God, humbled by this vision of His beloved Jewish multitudes. Not one among us understood the rags. We were all deeply moved, but we could only wonder what God meant by His "ragged, righteous remnant."

Chapter Ten

Winds of Change

The words are secret and sealed until the final period. Many shall be purified ... only the learners shall understand. Daniel 12:9-10

1965-1967: Cincinnati, Chattanooga, Lancaster, Indiana, Cincinnati

As time passed we continued to ponder the meaning of God's "ragged, righteous remnant," but our minds were also occupied by other things.

In early 1965, Marty and I realized that our associations were almost solely within the Christian community. As Jewish believers in the Messiah, we grieved to see that the older Hebrew Christians had almost no interaction with their Jewish neighbors. Marty and I realized that the message of the Jewish Messiah was for the entire Jewish community, not just people on the periphery. It had been that way in the Book of Acts. In one sense, we resided in both communities, but our ties to the Jewish community were limited. I longed to reestablish those ties by contributing to the community in some visible way.

I knew this would not be easy. I read in the Bible that it is harder for a rich man to be saved than for a camel to pass through the eye of a needle (Matthew 19:24). As I meditated on this astonishing fact, my eye skipped down two verses and caught the words, *"With men this is im-*

possible, but with God all things are possible" (Verses 26). I thought, *Even though it is very hard, humanly speaking, for wealthy people to become believers, the Lord can do it, and He will.* As I continued to meditate on this passage, a heavy burden came upon me for the mainstream Jewish people and I began to believe God for their salvation. This was something very new in its time. Very few believers were witnessing to the very heart and soul of the Jewish community.

I did have some close friends among elderly Jewish women. When one of them moved into Glen Manor, a progressive Reformed Jewish retirement center operated by The Home for Jewish Aged, I offered myself as a volunteer to help there wherever I was needed. I wanted the Jewish community to know that I not only loved the Jewish people and their souls, but I also cared for them as human beings with needs.

Although I explained that my husband was the leader of a Hebrew-Christian congregation, my offer to volunteer was accepted, and I began operating a little car pool for the elderly, driving them back and forth to wherever they needed to go. Eventually, the Glen Manor staff urged me to join the National Council of Jewish Women, which I did. I also became a member of both the Jewish Hospital volunteer staff and the B'nai B'rith Women.

One morning, I received a phone call from the head of the Glen Manor volunteers. She said that they wanted to start contributing a regular column to the weekly *American Israelite*, a local Jewish newspaper - vignettes from the lives of those who had made substantial donations to Glen Manor. She thought I might be the right person to handle the project. Would I be willing to interview the women concerned and write the columns, using my by-line, for the newspaper? she asked.

Incredibly, that very morning, I had prayed, generi-

Winds of Change

cally, for the lost sheep of the House of Israel and, specifically, for people in every strata of Jewish society to come to know their Messiah. And already the Lord was giving me the opportunity to meet some of those for whom I had prayed.

I eventually interviewed ten delightful men and women for the newspaper column. Each time, those being interviewed brought up the subject of my faith, asking me questions, which opened the door for me to tell them of our faith in *Yeshua* as the Jewish Messiah and of our congregation. The first woman I interviewed even canceled a board meeting so that we could continue talking. We talked together for more than two and a half hours. Who knows what God accomplished during those interviews?

In June 1965, we all attended the 50th (Jubilee) Conference of the Hebrew-Christian Alliance of America, held in Chattanooga, Tennessee. This proved to be a turning point for both the Chernoff family and the Alliance itself. We had attended these conferences occasionally, but they had seemed rather boring, even though we enjoyed the fellowship of other Jewish believers.

It was a unique organization, in that its members were encouraged to maintain a Jewish identity, to hold monthly or even weekly meetings in their respective cities, and to fellowship together, as Jews. The Alliance had been established in 1915; but, by the mid-60s, the organization was at a low ebb, definitely on the downswing. Marty and I both felt a deep desire to see this alliance prosper, to be a blessing to the Jewish community everywhere, so we agreed to commit ourselves to it, and to work with it over the next two years and to encourage the Jewish believers we knew to do the same. The next Alliance meeting was planned for 1967 to convene in Lancaster, Pennsylvania.

Born a Jew...Die a Jew

Those two years passed quickly, but just before the conference time rolled around, war broke out between Israel and her enemies. During the first weeks of June 1967, with breath held in abeyance and hearts pounding, we rode out the war, holding special, all-night prayer meetings. Marty and Al also attended and participated in emergency fund-raisers in the shocked, local Jewish community.

Breathlessly, we hung on to each news report. Israel had survived nineteen years of border raids by Arab neighbors from the north and east. Now Egypt had arbitrarily closed the Gulf of Aqaba to Israeli ships, and Arab armies were massing on every border. Finally, on June 5, Israel had struck back. Although she was outnumbered thirty to one, within just a few short days, Israel had completely destroyed the Arab air forces, defeated their ground troops, repossessed the Gaza Strip, the Sinai Peninsula, and the City of Jerusalem, and, finally, recaptured the Golan Heights. In six days the war was over.

We thrilled to accounts in Jewish newspapers of how even hard-hearted, atheistic Israelis reported miracles on the battlefield. There was no question about it: God had fought for Israel. Many Israelis on the scene were so moved that they were watching to see if Messiah would appear that very day. A few, of course, were giving all the credit to Israel's fearless army and air force. Many Jews around the world, however, truly, humbly believed that God Himself had once again saved Israel from annihilation. We were among them. One with the embattled Israelis in spirit, we gave God all the glory for their amazing victory, and praised Him mightily with singing, with raising and clapping our hands, with tears of joy and laughter.

Winds of Change

At the HCAA conference in Lancaster later that same month, we were all still basking in the afterglow of that great victory. In that atmosphere, Marty was asked to take a position on the Executive Board, a timely springboard of influence that would enable him to help shape the direction the Alliance would take in the future. The conference also attracted fifteen newly-saved, enthusiastic, young Jewish believers. One of them was Manny Brotman, a recent graduate of Moody Bible Institute's School of Jewish Studies. Mainly through the efforts of Manny and a few others, a youth branch of the Alliance, calling itself the Young Hebrew-Christian Alliance (YHCA), was officially formed, and Manny was elected as its president.

This proved to be a very timely innovation, since Jewish youth were being saved in visible numbers and were seeking fellowship with others like themselves. Having their own group, under the legal, protective umbrella of the HCAA, but with a separate constitution, helped bond the young people together with a true sense of their personal Jewish identification, as well as identification with each other as brothers and sisters in the Lord. All in all, the conference and its results proved to be very exciting.

We were looking forward to our twelfth trip to Indiana in August. We knew that everyone there would be celebrating Israel's prophetic victory in the Six Day War. Each summer, we had rejoiced with our Jewish friends over countless, newly-fulfilled prophecies concerning the Jewish people and the land of Israel, especially those concerning the restoration of the people of Israel to the land. Now, for the first time in nearly two thousand years, Jerusalem was again under Jewish control. On our way up from Cincinnati we felt a great excitement and could hardly wait to join the others in celebration.

Born a Jew...Die a Jew

The lovely conference grounds, located in a small village, had become as familiar to us as home, and the conferees were like family. But this time, everything was different.

When we arrived, we were greeted by an unprecedented and confused atmosphere. The Jewish believers assembled there appeared to be cowed by reports of Israel's victory, even embarrassed. The Gentile believers seemed to be almost angry with the brave, young little nation.

What was it? It couldn't have been the weather. The sun was seasonably warm, and the breeze from the lake was balmy. Something else was terribly lacking and it didn't take us long to identify it. There was no joy, no rejoicing over such an obvious response from God to the years of faithful intercession on the part of these people for Israel's victory over her mortal enemies who were furiously intent on driving her into the sea. We had been expecting celebration, but there was no celebration over such manifest fulfillment of God's prophecy concerning the Last Days and the soon return of Messiah to the earth.

Old, dear friends were reluctant even to discuss with us the still precarious position of little Israel. Their subtle withdrawal was as palpable as the heaviness of an approaching storm, and our hearts were wounded when we overheard whispered comments such as, "The victory was an out-and-out miracle of God."

"Those Jews better give God the glory and honor and credit. They better not claim it for themselves!"

"Those Jews better not be too jubilant!"

"Those Israelis better not be too proud!"

Their comments left me speechless. Marty was appalled and alarmed by the recognizable echoes of latent anti-Semitism. Until then, most of mainstream, evangelical Christianity had openly supported - even ap-

Winds of Change

plauded - the creation of the Jewish homeland in Palestine, "the land without a people" for "the people without a land."

By 1950, the world's wealthy nations - England, the United States and Canada included - had closed their doors to all future Jewish immigration, including survivors of the Holocaust. Incredibly, four years later, the General Assembly of the United Nations allocated $200 million for aid to the fewer than 900,000 Palestinian Arabs, who were, according to Basilea Schlink, in her book, *Israel, My Chosen People,* "the only refugees ever to be cared for and kept by International relief."

In 1958, Harry Golden recorded his astute observation for posterity, that, "Gentiles can shed crocodile tears in commiseration with the Jews, but... ***Jews must help themselves***" (emphasis mine).

And now, in 1967, at our familiar and beloved conference grounds in Indiana, Marty and I experienced this for ourselves. We had fully expected the conference leaders to tie the wonderful events of the Six Day War and all their ramifications with prophecies from both Covenants. Incredibly, not one speaker preached on it; not one teacher taught on it; not one person said anything about it to us.

Unaware that not even one, among the renowned theologians and prophetic scholars, had ever, even once, predicted that Jerusalem would be back in Jewish hands prior to the return of the Messiah at the very end of the Great Tribulation, we considered it to be a wonderful fulfillment of prophecy. All the scholars at that conference, however, played down the significance of Jerusalem returning to the Jews because it did not fit into their theology. Most of them were Scofield Dispensationalists who believed, according to Luke 21:24, which says, *"Jerusalem shall be trodden down of the Gentiles, until the times of the Gentiles be fulfilled"* (KJV), that this could only occur after the Church was raptured out of the world and before the Great Tribulation Period. The fact that Jerusalem had already returned to Jewish rule meant to them that the "Times of the Gentiles" had already ended, and that threw their theology into disarray.

Amazingly, some of these "experts on Bible prophecy" argued that, since the Temple Mount was still in the hands of the Arabs (Gentiles), control of the city by the Jews could not be of any prophetic significance!

The Jewish believers among us were not much better. It almost felt to us as though they were ashamed of what had happened in Israel. We could not have known that the ultimate outcome of this remarkable prophecy would be the beginning of the spiritual restoration of the Jewish people, but we did sense that it was very important, too important to ignore.

When I questioned one of the Jewish Bible scholars about the abrupt change in mood, he shook his head. "Sorry to say, Joanna, it's a phenomenon. It's just very difficult for non-Jews to get excited over something good and wonderful happening to the Jews. They say they love Israel and are moved by looking at pictures of pitiful, starving Jewish babies and other Holocaust victims. They root for the underdog. But, when the Jewish people rise up and God begins to work in their behalf, something strange happens, something incomprehensible. I'm sorry, but that's what you are seeing and feeling right here among your old friends."

This sudden breach, like a death in the family, shook Marty and me to the core, and began to affect us very deeply. We discerned a chilling lack of sympathy, a disturbing isolation of the Jewish believers, by the Gentile believers, whom we had counted on as friends of the Jews. It made us recall Harry Golden's words: "Jews

Winds of Change

must help themselves." Marty and I both felt the same chill all over the conference grounds. Our Gentile Christian friends could not rejoice with us over the victory of our people.

One evening, while Marty and our children were outside on the conference grounds, I went inside the little restaurant where we got our sodas and snacks and sat down at the piano. More to lift my own spirits than anything else, I began playing and singing some of the original, lively, new Yiddish and Israeli songs we so enjoyed in our services at home. Soon, a very irate man stomped over to me and demanded, "What do you think you're doing, putting Christian words to such worldly music? If you're going to play anything, play hymns, something that honors the Lord!" He glared at me, turned his back, and stalked away.

I sat there stunned from such an unexpected rebuke, not having realized how unacceptable Jewish music was at that time to the Gentile world. A man who overheard what was said came over to me quickly and said, "Don't pay any attention to him! A lot of our English hymns come from German military-marching songs. Some were even drinking songs! You go ahead. Play what you've been playing. It's beautiful."

This encouragement came too late. I no longer had the heart to play anymore. Sobered by the sudden overall change in the spiritual climate, Marty and I both began to realize just how thoroughly Jewish we were, that, after all, Gentiles are Gentiles, and Jews are Jews. Although both are equally cherished in God's heart, and both are vital to His unfolding drama of human events, they are very different.

We had rounded a corner and come suddenly upon the end of a road, a predestined turning point. We were still trusting that God's hand was leading us, but we were totally in the dark about how these events would eventually culminate. Consciously and emotionally we were being separated, not from the universal Body of believers in *Yeshua* the Messiah, but from the structured, Gentile-Church establishment. It was time. Sadly, we gathered our three children and our little Jewish flock, and drove home.

Back home in Cincinnati, Marty and I cried out to God, "Why, O God? We don't understand! Why are our friends suddenly no longer friends of Israel? All this time they've been sympathetic and supportive. Why now so cold? Because Israel won the War? Are her long-standing friends no longer friends because the feeble, suffering, disadvantaged, heroic little underdog, the poor, emaciated Holocaust victim has helped herself? Does Christian compassion stretch only as far as our misery and helplessness as a people?"

We could not have known at the time that the chilly winds that swept through the conference were but an emerging trend. Soon the evidence became all too clear. Everywhere, a large slice of mainstream, evangelical Christianity resented Israel's overwhelming victory.

With this turn of events, Marty disappeared (as was his custom) into his private study, to fast and to pray before the Lord. Soon, he emerged refreshed, confident, fully convinced, as were most of the Jewish believers, that the Six Day War was unquestionably a prophetic milestone for the Jewish people and Jewish believers in *Yeshua* alike. God was in control.

Recalling the few encouraging words I received at the conference about my music, I once again sat down at the piano and began improvising. This time, instead of writing Christian sentiments to old Yiddish tunes, I turned it around and wrote "Messianic" words to melodies from the old, traditional-hymns, unaware that I was

Winds of Change

composing the very first of a new type of worship song that God would use to enhance the as-yet-unidentified "new thing" He was doing.

Later that summer, while home alone one night, I had been reading Leon Uris' book, *Exodus,* and praying for a deeper work of the Holy Spirit in my life. I laid the book aside, recalling the first two wonderful times when the Holy Spirit had dealt with the issues of my life: first, in 1948, when as a young girl in the Nazarene Church I had yielded my all to Him; then, again, in 1960, when Marty and I prayed together for a new infilling, and we both received the gift of tongues.

That night, for the third time, our gracious Lord infused me with His Spirit, this time with an overwhelming, total transformation of my inner man, as if "born a Jew," ardently Zionistic in both identification and perspective, fanatical, with a "holy bias" which would last me the rest of my life. I came out of the experience even more radically Jewish-minded than my Jewish husband was at the time.

Inspired by an almost obsessive fervency for Yiddish, Israeli and Zionist music, I began teaching our adults and children many wonderful, musical Yiddish words and phrases. I was overjoyed when another woman in our fellowship began teaching our children, who attended Bible school, the Hebrew alphabet. We were moving our Hebrew-Christian congregation into a culturally Jewish way of worship.

My heart, therefore, was deeply stirred when Marty said to me, "Joanna, I believe that God is calling me to greater commitment and identification with my own people. When I see so many biblical prophecies being fulfilled - the bloody battlefields in the Middle East, Jerusalem now back in the Jewish hands after more than 1900 years - praise our Almighty God, I believe He is about to lead us in a new direction. I do not see it clearly yet. But, if we continue to seek His will, He will show us, and we will know when He does."

Marty was right. God did eventually show us. But the "new thing" He was creating, calling us and our family to pioneer for Him, would come only gradually into focus over the next four years. Then, persecution, by those who didn't understand what God was doing, would begin in earnest.

Chapter Eleven

A New Thing Coming

Whom will He teach knowledge, and who shall be made to understand the message? Babes just weaned from the milk, just drawn from the breasts?   Isaiah 28:9

1967: Cincinnati

The activities of our ministry - forming a congregation in our home, composing worship songs to old Jewish music, identifying socially with the Jewish community, witnessing directly to the families and friends of Jewish believers, going back to our Jewish roots - all estranged us to some degree, not only from some of the Gentile Christians, but even from certain Jewish believers, as well. These were "Hebrew Christians" staunchly entrenched in the Church with no desire to rock the boat. They warned us that we were becoming "too Jewish," that we were "building up a middle wall of partition" between Jew and Gentile. It was certainly not our intention to separate ourselves from the Body of believers, but simply to express our worship in our own cultural ways, as no longer an integral part of the denominational Church system, but remaining, spiritually, one with them in the Body of the Messiah. We therefore did not break off our relationship with the organization we had served so many years, despite the disappointing experience we had at the conference following the Six Day War and despite the fact that we were often called on the carpet because of our fledgling Hebrew-Christian, admittedly charismatic congregation.

Even though the president had personally given us free reign to work in our own way in our own city, he had gently but often reminded us of an obvious truth. I could not quote him exactly, but the message was clearly as follows, "We appreciate how successful you are, bringing new Jewish believers to the conference each year. However, we do not approve of your having your own congregation. As we have told you before, you should plant all your Jewish believers into a local Christian church, where they can put down roots, be assimilated, and establish their identities as Christians."

In spite of the fact that we resisted this counsel, he knew how dedicated we were, and, because he liked us personally, kept us on staff. Because of the fellowship we enjoyed with the group, and, admittedly, the financial stability their salary provided us, we stayed with them. However, when the president of the organization died in the mid-60s, he was succeeded by a non-Jewish leader, who was even less tuned in to how God was moving among the Jewish people. He objected strenuously to our separate congregation, and, especially, to our discipling methods. After he assumed authority, we had to tread lightly, as if on egg shells.

It was the Lord Himself who was turning us, moving us, pushing us in an entirely new direction, and we simply could not turn back from the direction He was revealing to us. Had we been totally comfortable in any church, had we been sufficiently supported, emotionally and financially, by any church, any denomination, or any mission board, perhaps we would never have realized the new thing God was seeking to accomplish through and in us, never have been willing to take the

A New Thing Coming

giant steps of faith He required of us. He was however, already encouraging our hearts with a direct word:

> *A voice is calling, "Clear the way for the* LORD *in the wilderness; make straight in the desert a highway for our God. ... The crooked turns must be straightened, and all the rough places made smooth. The glory of the Lord shall be revealed ... .* Isaiah 40:3-5

Marty was both humbled and thrilled to be pastoring his people, and greatly relieved to have a permanent place, even a recreation room, to bring Jewish believers and seekers to fellowship. They needed a place where they felt comfortable and at ease, where they could ask whatever questions were on their minds and hearts, where they could, more openly and freely, explore their Jewishness and their Jewish roots. To us, making disciples meant more than saving souls, it meant saving lives.

Family-salvation principles, which God was building into our ministry, were being firmly established on Scripture. We believed absolutely that, throughout the Bible, God dealt with families as single units, that when one person became a believer, the family members were spiritually (but not automatically) "sanctified" to the Lord, "set aside" in a supernatural way, to be saved. *"Believe on the Lord Jesus Christ,"* the Scriptures say, *"and you will be saved, **your family also**"* (Acts 16:31, emphasis mine). Working from this principle, we devoted much time to the friends and families of new believers.

Our foundation stones were tested and proven. After the field was first cleared of intellectual debate, and unbelief was rooted out and rejected, the stones were laid: 1) love, the main thing; 2) the Holy Spirit, our source of power; 3) prayer and fasting in the Spirit, thereby bringing God's will to fruition; 4) unwavering and expectant faith in God for the End-time harvest of Jewish souls; 5) salvation for entire families; 6) a growing Jewish identity; 7) Jewish congregations; and 8) Jewish music about the Messiah *Yeshua*.

We put a great emphasis on hospitality, seeking always to have an open door to people coming and going, sharing meals, prayer meetings, Bible studies, children's meetings, friendship and personal ministry to any and all. Fervent prayer, bathed in love, would cover us.

For Pastor and Mrs. Martin Chernoff and family, no matter where the road might lead at this point, there was no turning back.

Meanwhile, somewhere out there in God's wide world something else, something new and momentous, was astir.

Chapter Twelve

A Crossroads

Sing unto the Lord a new song.
Sing, O barren… .
Then shall the virgin [Israel] rejoice in the dance… .
I will turn their mourning into joy.
                    Isaiah 42:10, 54: and Jeremiah 31:13

1968-1969: Cincinnati

By 1968, the social climate of the nation was in upheaval. It was a time for radical leftist politics, the communistic Students for a Democratic Society inciting campus riots, revolution and race riots, the counterculture, hippies and dropouts, marches, demonstrations, draft-card and flag burning, marijuana and LSD, uppers and downers, Martin Luther King, Jr., Woodstock and the Chicago Democratic Convention.

At the same time, the spiritual climate was also in upheaval. Like a sleeping volcano, first there was a rumbling centered inthe Haight-Asbury district of San Francisco. Then such an eruption burst upon the horizon - a spiritual tidal wave, flooding the nation from west to east - that only Almighty God Himself could have planned and executed.

Thousands upon thousands of young drug addicts, dropouts, runaways, flower children, rebels with and without causes "turned on" to Jesus, becoming Street Christians, Jesus People, Jesus Freaks, the Jesus Revolution, the Jesus Generation. They were swept up in whirlwinds of praise and prayer and holy adoration of the Son of God. As one, they fell in love with God's Anointed, Jesus of Nazareth, King of Kings, Lord of Lords, Savior of the World. Among them, multitudes of Jewish youth "turned on" to the same and only Savior, Jesus the Messiah, King of the Jews, King of the Universe.

As the wave swept across America, new, small Bible studies in homes, in empty buildings and in warehouses sprang up independently, apart from the established, formal churches - an antiestablishment street-movement of dissatisfied, uprooted, restless, young people - Protestants, Catholics, Jews, most of them unchurched, and many self-avowed atheists and anarchists - accepting Jesus, telling other young people, even forming religious communes.

Masses of young Jewish people from religious and nonreligious families were born again by the Spirit of God. Some joined huge churches - Melodyland in Santa Clara, for example, that soon hired four Jewish assistant pastors. Others began frequenting synagogues for the first time in their lives.

Life Magazine wrote that the churches that recognized this as a move of God and opened up their doors, got blessed and revived. If they did not, it passed them by. Each member of the *Life* team that went to cover the Jesus Movement in California, according to reports, came back home a staunch believer in Jesus. Some parents were quoted as saying that they would rather have their kids on drugs than caught up in such "fanaticism." Drug addiction apparently was something they could more easily understand.

When the spiritual fallout hit Cincinnati in 1968-69, we were astonished to see so many young Jewish people

A Crossroads

suddenly on fire for God. But why should we have been surprised? We had prayed for years for just such a revival. Still, we were taken aback that so many of them were strange-looking hippies, dressed either in long, tattered skirts or dirty, ragged jeans and tee-shirts, with head-bands, torn sandals on dirty feet, scraggly long hair or "afros," in all shades and colors, with beads and leather laces, just off marijuana and LSD and other drugs: members of God's own redeemed "ragged righteous remnant," fulfillment of Marty's second major, puzzling, yet thrilling vision. Here they were - in the flesh.

A very stable member of our congregation brought her hippie son to one of our meetings. A leader in his high school, in both drug abuse and political activism, he gave his heart to Jesus. He was also delivered from his addiction to LSD. The next day he brought two friends with him, a Jew and a Gentile, who in turn surrendered their lives to the Lord. These three became so zealous, so on fire for God, they breathed new life into our youth group, and helped us break through some of our own conventional, establishment, old Hebrew-Christian-tradition hang-ups. We began to want them in our midst dressed as they were, in their blue jeans, tee-shirts and sandals, with their long scraggly hair and beards, seated on our floor with their eyes closed, strumming their guitars and crooning Scriptures to their gentle music.

Meanwhile, Joel and David, both musically talented, had already gained a wonderful, classical education in music from their first piano teacher. Their second and last teacher, with an entirely different approach, expected them to spend long hours doing finger exercises. But I often heard Joel at the piano getting off on his own jazzy innovations instead, and it made me uneasy. When I complained to Joel's teacher, she agreed to speak to him, and I heard no more about it.

Later that spring, Marty and I attended her recital, which consisted of all her students, including Joel, playing some of his original compositions. While it sounded strange to us, the audience loved it. Afterwards, the teacher repeated my complaint to the audience, then added, "Joel is a very talented young man with an ear for classical jazz. His original compositions are so technically perfect, one would have to graduate from the conservatory to accomplish what he does naturally. He has a talent from God."

I leaned over and whispered to Marty, "Maybe something's going on here. Maybe we shouldn't be uptight about this. Maybe he has a gift."

Marty whispered back, "I don't know. It's too modern for me."

When I questioned Joel later, he explained to me that the sound was "contemporary," a term I did not quite understand. He was writing songs about the Lord not to be "spiritual," but because it was "cool." He also assured me that the sound was here to stay.

Joel and David, both active members of Youth For Christ, had organized a choral group, and were entering state and national Youth For Christ competitions. At a local competition, Joel won hands-down in the solo category, and the choral group won in the choral category. But this caused a problem. Joel was disqualified after the fact (no reason given) and replaced as winner by someone else. Later, one outraged member of the judges' panel told us what happened. One of the other judges complained, "Why should we give all the honors to the Jews? They're taking over here!" Others on the panel agreed, and the honor was then transferred to a non-Jewish competitor. All we, as Joel's parents, could

A Crossroads

do was sigh and grieve silently for him in our hearts. The "middle wall of partition" separating between Jew and Gentile, one way or the other, still stood with its many faces, indeed a formidable barrier.

Undaunted, a short time later, Joel and some friends put a little band together, and they practiced in our basement. Instead of playing improvisations of church music, which I expected to hear, they "jammed," making that contemporary sound again, the sound that made me uneasy. One day, from the top of the stairs, I called down to them, "What is that, Christian rock?" Little did I realize that my intended irony was prophetic.

Joel continued to compose his own music. As a result, when "Jesus coffee houses" began springing up in Cincinnati, the only person in town with music appropriate for the coffee house crowd was Joel. In the first coffee house to open, on the very first night, he played an original composition, entitled *Heaven or Hell.* Later, when someone gave an invitation to accept Jesus, seven young people; moved by the message of Joel's music, repented of their sins, and gave their hearts to the Lord.

Once again, I had to acknowledge that the Holy Spirit was working in ways I did not understand. I had to witness it first hand in my own son before I stopped *nudging* (nagging) him to play only what sounded right to me.

At the June 1969 HCAA conference, held in Asheville, North Carolina, the youth contingent was growing. Joe Finkelstein came from Philadelphia. Itwas Joe's first time to attend, and he was promptly elected president of the Youth Alliance.

A delightful though disturbing crisis occurred one day, when we were waiting in the cafeteria for lunch. Someone from our group said, "Let's sing a song!" In response, we all began to sing, *Havenu shalom aleichem,* an old Hebrew folk song the older Hebrew Christians present would all surely remember from their childhood. And sing it we did, with energy, enthusiasm and joy.

Abruptly, some of the older Hebrew Christians' Gentile wives accosted us. "Why are you singing that? Don't you know you shouldn't sing Jewish songs!"

Their sudden anger amazed us. What could be wrong with enjoying a simple, little song familiar to all Jewish people from ages past? After all, we were all still Jews. But the older Hebrew Christians were embarrassed and rushed to suppress our singing. How assimilated they were! How far removed from their own people! I wondered, sadly, just how they would explain the scriptural teaching that admonishes the believer to *"remain in the calling in which he was called"* (1 Corinthians 7:20, NKJ); and which of us was the more legalistic?

In August, at the annual conference in Indiana, several members of our home group, who had recently been saved, wanted to be immersed, and they asked Marty to immerse them in the lake. Since immersion was recognizably a type of the Jewish *mikvah* (purification bath) from the Torah, he happily immersed them all one-by-one, "in the name of the Father, the Son, and the Holy Spirit." He had not foreseen that there would be any problem.

When the head of the organization heard about it, he saw red. According to his persuasion, Marty had absolutely no authority to immerse anyone. We were never to repeat the offense. We were only to bring any new believers to the local churches where they would be immersed by ordained, denominational pastors. We were then to step aside - or be fired! Once again, they questioned our right to hold congregational meetings at our home, even though we were diligent to send all monies

A Crossroads

collected immediately to headquarters, and they used those funds to pay our salary.

The organizational leadership kept hammering at us: "Why do you have this congregation meeting in your home? Why aren't you rooting your Jewish believers in the local churches?" It seemed to us that they never mentioned anything else, especially anything we might have been doing well. Apparently, nothing we did could please them. I soon came to believe that Marty's affinity with Charles Finney was based on the knowledge that Finney, in his generation, was often misunderstood and, consequently, experienced his greatest attacks from other believers. The situation was again coming to a head.

Still, God was. blessing us. One day I returned home from shopping, unlocked the front door, turned the knob, and tried to open the door, but it seemed to be stuck. Something was barring it from the inside, preventing me from entering my own home. I pushed harder, and finally was able to get the door open far enough that I could squeeze through. The "something" turned out to be live bodies, seated all over the floor, even up against the door. Our living room and dining room were both wall-to-wall with young people - Jewish and Gentile both, spiritually hungry hippies, who had heard about us from somewhere, and had come to our house to find out from Marty how to get saved!

Marty and I were honored to be loving these young people, presenting the claims of *Yeshua* the Messiah to them, leading them through repentance to salvation. Marty thrived, thrilled and humbled that God had called him to just such a congregation as this "ragged, righteous remnant," with their open hearts and open minds, hungry for new lives in the Messiah.

Our own boys, who considered themselves to be nominal believers, were, at the time, students at the University of Cincinnati. They had been raised as believers, they professed salvation, and they came to services; but, to them, it was old hat. They were no longer excited or thrilled about their experience. As I compared them with the recently reborn Jesus People, I began to wonder if maybe it was better to be saved in the Jesus Revolution than to be as spiritually dry as our young people seemed to be. On the other hand, Hope, our tenderhearted nine-year-old, made a strong affirmation of faith, declaring to God that she never wanted to be separated from Him - not now, not ever.

So, we walked in tenuous confidence, from one day to the next, in awe of the ways in which God was moving among us, using such a phenomenon as our congregation. Our Jewish believers were not being assimilated into denominational churches, not losing their identity as Jews, not losing their concern for their own people. And we believed that God was pleased by that.

Then one day, in the fall of 1969, Marty got a phone call from the new head of the organization who questioned him about why we were not sending in our monthly work sheets, not distributing their literature, not visiting stores or knocking on doors. Marty tried to explain: "We are already heavily involved in personal work. We just don't have the time. Check our records and see what's been happening here: Dozens of young people are getting saved. We're leading Jewish people to salvation in the Lord all the time. We are the only ones who come every year to the summer conference bringing new believers with us. The way we're doing the work, works for us. You know how successful we are."

After a grim pause, Marty hung up the phone. "Another clash," he said to me.

"What did he say?"

A Crossroads

"He said, 'Maybe you shouldn't be so successful. Maybe you should be doing what we tell you to do.' Joanna, he sounded much less interested in whether any Jewish people are becoming believers, than in whether we are doing our work their way."

"That's not really what they're upset about," I said. "They resent your pastoring this little Jewish congregation."

"Well, I'm sorry," he said. "God's leading has been clearly in that direction, so that is not going to change. We cannot turn back."

Little did we know that we had come to the most critical juncture, literally a crossroads in our ministry that would change our lives forever.

CHAPTER THIRTEEN

THE THIRD VISION – MESSIANIC JUDAISM

I and the children whom the Lord has given me ... are for signs and wonders in Israel. Isaiah 8:18, KJV

1970: CINCINNATI, OAK PARK, INDIANA, CINCINNATI

We had been wounded by the prejudice we discerned in many of the churches, and the occasional anti-Semitic remarks made by some members. These occasions always drove us to the Lord, and we would ask Him, "Why is this happening?" The Lord would always comfort our hearts with His response:

> *I am creating something new in the spiritual realm. Many - not all believers - whose hearts do not fully discern My love for My people Israel, are not aware that this is a move of My Spirit.*

This made us to realize that we were standing on the threshold of something great, something far beyond our own unique congregation. We were rapidly moving into a period of powerful spiritual revival in the earth.

Almost every attempt by Hebrew Christians in the past to form congregations of Jewish believers had failed. Among the few notable exceptions was a congregation founded in Illinois in 1934, the First Hebrew-Presbyterian Church of Chicago, pastored by David Bronstein,

Born a Jew...Die a Jew

Sr., under the auspices of the Presbyterian Church, USA. But David had to work to justify the use of the word "Hebrew" in the name, stressing that the liturgy was not patterned after that of the synagogue, but merely sprinkled with a few colorful Hebrew phrases and the reciting of the *Sh'ma*. While there were a few other isolated incidents of congregations of Jewish believers, most were more along the lines of a Jewish church rather than a synagogue and were an extension. of the Christian church at large.: Consequently, most .Jewish members ultimately assimilated into the church, along with most other Jewish believers at this time, and were soon lost to their people.

Their attempts, however, were still vitally important for future generations, because they expressed that deep need within Jewish followers of *Yeshua* to remain Jewish and to have their own congregations. It is this deep-rooted desire that would be the hallmark of the future movement of Messianic Judaism. No doubt others, who had tried, failed because it was not yet within God's prophetic timetable for them to flourish.

In early 1970, we relocated our crowded Sunday morning worship services and our Tuesday night prayer meetings to the large Community Room of the Standard Building and Loan Company, in the suburb of Pleasant Ridge. Shortly thereafter, Marty received his third powerful vision from the Lord: two electrifying, simple words stretched across the sky in the form of a banner, bringing into focus and confirming what we had been sensing over the years: ***MESSIANIC JUDAISM***

Once this ideal, this motto, this goal, became implanted in his spirit, it became a force in his life, his main topic of conversation, his sole purpose for living. Convinced that it was entirely of God, he never faltered in its pursuit.

The Third Vision-Messianic Judaism

Our congregation felt that it was time for us to rise up as one body to make a statement. In effect, we agreed that: "We are Jewish believers in *Yeshua* as our Messiah. We have our own destiny in the Lord. We will no longer be assimilated into the church and pretend to be non-Jews. If *Yeshua* Himself, His followers and the early Jewish believers tenaciously maintained their Jewish lifestyles, why was it right then, but wrong now? Gentile converts are not expected to forsake their families, cultures, holidays and traditions; nor shall we do so.

"We will raise our children to be consciously aware at all times that they are Jewish, with a special calling to be a part of their own people and to win them to Messiah. Instead of celebrating traditional Christian holidays, we will start honoring biblical Jewish holy days, those that God Himself established for us to honor for everlasting generations, and we will do so by choice, not as compelled."

We believed that God Himself was saving Jewish people, giving them hearts to be Jewish in their identification - a visible remnant to fulfill Bible prophecy of the Last Days. They would be the believing remnant of Israel, Jewish people going back to the Land, back to their roots, back to their own people, back to their God. We also believed that God wanted our son and our daughter to marry other Jewish believers whenever possible. To some, it sounded prejudicial, but it was not. I myself am not Jewish by birth. It is a matter of a calling. The children born into our family are called to be part and parcel of our calling to the Jewish people. While we recognized that there were non-Jews like myself who had a calling like Ruth, we felt that our children should marry Jewish believers if at all possible.

Because of this conviction, we began to speak to them

early in their dating lives about such a calling, going out of our way to drive them to other cities to attend conferences where they would meet other young "Messianic Jewish" youth, like themselves. We sought to make the things of the Lord exciting to them. Whatever sacrifice that entailed on our part, we were glad to do it.

It seemed incredible to us that many of the older Hebrew Christians were digging in their heels against the innovations of the young, taking their stand, like the denominational churches had, for the most part, against the invasion of the hippies. They could not see that this was a sovereign move of God.

Marty and I were, apparently, the only older workers ministering among Jewish people, truly moving forward with the Jesus Movement at the time, recognizing that the youth were the future of revival.

That fall, still puzzled by the old-line Hebrew Christians who were willing to retain only a surface Jewishness, and were defensively content being assimilated into the churh, I went back to school at the University of Cincinnati, enrolling in several race and relationship courses. When I soon discovered that many of the most radical and violent students on campus were Jewish, I began attending their meetings, believing that they were actually searching for answers to life, just as I, too, had explored politics as a young girl. I made a point of befriending those who claimed to be open to radical religious and political ideas, literally following them around campus, and inviting some of them home to dinner.

What a dramatic turnaround this represented in our approach to ministry! We went from a normal, rather ordinary ministry, to having this amazing, steady stream of hippies, campus radicals, and anti-American activists coming to our house-young Jewish people coming to

The Third Vision-Messianic Judaism

us with their miraculous stories of how their lives had been changed. It was thrilling, like being vicariously born again over and over, watching the fulfillment of our prayers, always acutely aware that we were not making it happen, fully aware that God alone was supernaturally creating "something new" around us.

The parents of Johnny, the miraculously healed, formerly-comatose boy Marty had prayed for in the hospital, were the wealthy owners of a restaurant chain. They had already stopped attending their old church, and soon started coming, with their children, to our meetings. Their former pastor complained loudly to the head of the organization with which we worked about the defection of the family. For the leadership of the organization, it was the last straw.

The head of the organization wrote us a letter that said in effect, "As we have reminded you many times in the past, when your Jewish people become believers, you are required to take them and leave them in a local church. The ordained minister of that church can disciple them, not you. At this time, you are required to do the following: First, disburse the congregation that meets in your home; then appear in person here at headquarters with a complete list of the names and addresses of all your so-called members, with complete records of all offerings received. We need to know exactly what you are doing there in Cincinnati."

From the tone of his letter, we understood that, in order to continue moving in the direction the Lord was leading us, we had to resign. Either that, or stay bound by our salary to the mission, trying to appease them. We had a choice to make, and we had to make it quickly. We called for a special meeting of the entire congregation (about 30-40 at that time) and laid the specifics out before them.

Born a Jew...Die a Jew

The congregation was told by some of the leadership, "We're at a crossroads. We cannot continue as we are. Either we disband as a congregation so Marty and Joanna can continue being supported by the organization, or Marty resigns from the organization and becomes our full-fledged pastor-rabbi. If that's what we decide we really want, we'll have to support them like any other pastor - with a living wage."

The congregation was stunned. Such a concept was acceptable in the Christian church, but absolutely unheard of for a Jewish congregation at the time, completely contrary to anything and everything being said and done in any outreach ministry to the Jewish people anywhere.

To our knowledge, except for the rare and isolated exception over centuries, no one else had ever tried what we were getting ready to do. We were praying about establishing an independent Messianic Jewish congregation, a synagogue, if you will, totally self-supporting and free from all official ties to the Christian establishment. The monumental and historical scope of this proposal was both breathtaking and scary.

We have never tried to take credit for Messianic Judaism and Messianic synagogues or even to state that we were the first Messianic synagogue of this Movement. Others were being stirred to move in the same direction at about the same time. When we came to this crossroads, however, and looked around to ask someone else if we were on the right track or were completely *"meshugge"* (crazy) for persisting in this endeavor, we found no one to ask. Alone, Marty considered and prayed over the three wondrous visions he had received from the Lord: The first, in 1948, of endless orchards ripe for the harvest, which he understood to mean a vast revival among Jewish youth.

The Third Vision-Messianic Judaism

The second, in 1963, of those same Jewish youth, God's "ragged, righteous remnant."

The third, early in 1970, of the astonishing banner emblazoned across the sky, proclaiming MESSIANIC JUDAISM, which we still did not fully understand.

Altogether, they comprised one tremendous revelation: Multitudes of straggling, ragamuffin, young, Jewish youth, coming to a saving knowledge of *Yeshua* as their long-awaited Messiah, gathered together by God Himself under a banner that no man had ever known before "Messianic Judaism." There was not the slightest doubt in Marty's heart that God was leading him into this new and independent "Messianic" ministry. But was the timing right?

There were many other questions. Privately, Al Adler, our close friend, asked Marty, "Is that what you really want?"

Marty and I both knew that, before we launched out independently upon such a gigantic undertaking, we needed to hear from God directly, so we took a few days off to fast and pray. "Heavenly Father," we prayed, "what do *You* want us to do? We are so tired of being poor. Constant concern about finances keeps us ineffectual. If we try to live by faith, somehow or other, our faith is not what it should be, and we suffer as a result. If we remain with the organization, we will be tied to a structure that does not work for us. Show us what *You* want us to do, which way *You* want us to go."

The Lord showed us in His Word:

You cannot serve God and mammon [money]. ... Do not, then, be anxious. Your heavenly father knows [what] you need . ... But you, seek first His kingdom and His righteousness and all these things will be added to you.   Matthew 6:24-33

Born a Jew...Die a Jew

Later, alone, but still on my knees by the bed, I read two astonishing passages from the Bible:

> *Know thoroughly the condition of your flocks; keep your mind on your herds ... . The lambs are for your clothing; the goats furnish money for a field. There will be enough goat's milk for your food, for the food of your household, and a living for your maidens.*
> *The vessels ... are bringing your sons from afar; their silver and gold is with them ... .*
> Proverbs 27:23, 26-27 and Isaiah 60:9

"Lord," I prayed, "are You saying that, if we concentrate all our attention on the ministry You have given us, that our spiritual sons and daughters will bring in their silver and gold to support us?"

Marty and I studied those Scriptures together. There was nobody else around to ask. We would be paving the way without having anyone to turn to for "advice and consent," except the Lord. We talked it over, prayed, and finally decided: yes, it really was God. He was moving us out, "by faith," to pastor an indigenous, self-supporting congregation of Messianic Jews - a phenomenon in the world. It did not feel like a phenomenon. How could we know that the Messianic Movement would grow and spread throughout the world?

We had no way of knowing that God was already stirring hearts among our youth and the older believers to support us with tithes and offerings. After we announced our decision to go for it, one young girl, who had been a believer for only about a year, told me that the Lord had instructed her to contribute $5,000, the most we had ever received from one person in our lives.

Believing that God had confirmed our decision, instead of driving up to headquarters to submit to the

The Third Vision-Messianic Judaism

organization's stringent form of legalistic control, in early October 1970, we submitted our second and final letter of resignation.

Later that same month, back home in Cincinnati, we incorporated "Congregation *Beth* Messiah," to the best of our knowledge, both then and now, possibly the first modern, indigenous, independent, self-supporting, self-propagating Messianic Jewish congregation in the United States.

Chapter Fourteen

THE PRAYER MEETING

I will render useless the wisdom of the learned and set aside the understanding of the intelligent ... . God has chosen the world's foolish things to put to shame the learned.   1 Corinthians 1:19, 27

1970-1971: CINCINNATI

One evening, in the late fall of 1970, while I was away visiting in Atlanta, Marty was upstairs in our bedroom, reading behind closed doors. The house was otherwise deserted, when for some reason sixteen of our young people - some believers, but not all - came in together. Joel and David and a few of our young people, who were already stirred up by the spiritual revival of the Jesus Movement going on around them, had been having heavy "rap" sessions and asking questions that apparently had no answers, at least, not to their satisfaction. Nobody remembers why, but they had decided to have a prayer meeting at our house.

David, who was nineteen, confessed later that, at that time, he "identified as a believer" but felt cold and very rebellious, almost angry, concerning spiritual matters. Often Marty had challenged David in his faith, even getting so exasperated with him that he would state bluntly, "David, I don't think you're saved. I'm afraid if you die, you'll go to hell. You have never had a real taste of the Lord." David would relate later that these talks just made him madder. The rebelliousness of the age had gotten hold of him.

Even though David had been touched by the articles on the Jesus Movement, he still did not want to be at that prayer meeting. He was there simply because it was happening in his own home. Joel, who was twenty, was also there. Thirteen-year-old Hope had joined them, expecting a little prayer meeting, followed by a big party.

Since no one among the sixteen crowded into our small living room knew what to do, they decided to separate into two rooms. David stayed with seven others in the living room, Joel and Hope went with the rest into the back den.

David knelt on the floor with his head on the sofa, hoping to fall asleep. Suddenly he felt a stirring in his spirit and heard a voice like a clear bell: *Go over there and pray for that girl.* The girl was a 13-year-old drug user from a very wealthy family. David remembers that something just seemed to lift him off his knees supernaturally and start him walking toward the girl. Simultaneously, others were being led to pray for this young girl. He went over to the girl, intending to place his hands on her shoulders and to pray for her. At the same time, Joel in the other room was prompted by the Spirit to approach a young boy across the room and pray for him.

At the precise moment that David in the one room reached the girl, and Joel, in the other room, reached the boy, the Holy Spirit of God burst in upon both groups like an ocean overwhelming the shore, one tidal wave of glory after another, rolling over and over and over them all. All were filled - every one of them in both rooms - to overflowing with the Holy Spirit, touched by the *Shekinah* (presence) of God - just as the Jewish disciples had experienced it in Acts 2. As one, they leapt to their feet. They wept, they laughed, they shouted,

The Prayer Meeting

jumped up and down, hugged one another, prayed for each other, screamed praises to God, pounded the walls with their fists, and continued doing so for seven, eight, nine hours without stopping.

Upstairs, Marty, startled to his feet by the sudden explosive roar and pounding, flew down the stairs to see what earth-shaking event was taking place in his home. When he realized, astonished, that it was the all-consuming presence of the *Ruach HaKodesh,* and that all the young people, all ecstatic, were assuredly in their right minds, he asked quietly, "Are you all right?"

"Yes! Praise God! Hallelujah!"

"Yes! Hallelujah! Thank You, *Yeshua!*"

"Yes! Yes! Yes!"

Awestruck by what he had both seen and heard, he retreated backwards up the stairs to listen, to praise, to pray, and to meditate on the incredible blessing from God the young people were experiencing right underneath his feet. When he later came back downstairs, he hardly recognized them, so radiant were they with the glory of God.

When I returned home later that week, I too hardly recognized my own children. All three had an Acts-Two experience and done glorious things in the Spirit, things which they had never done before. Their faces were aglow with the Spirit, shining like Moses' face when he came back down from Mt. Sinai after having been in the very presence of God (Exodus 34:29-30).

The results were startling and permanent. From then on, the entire group of heretofore unsaved or, at best, nominal believers, were on fire for God. Whenever they weren't glued to their Bibles, they were all over town as our representatives of the counterculture, "Jewish Jesus Freaks," with their long hair, jeans and sandals, witnessing in the power of the Spirit to addicts and pushers,

Born a Jew...Die a Jew

hippies and policemen - anyone who would listen, but mainly to the hippies. While the hippies were high on drugs, our kids were high on *Yeshua.*

The instantaneous, amazing change in each one of the sixteen young people was characterized by a gnawing hunger for God and an insatiable thirst for His Word. As they pored over the Scriptures, for the first time seeing religious practices in the *Tanach,* in the light of the *Brit Hadashah,* they were astounded by the inherent Jewishness of the Messiah *Yeshua* and his followers.

Every day, for six months, they gathered, first for prayer, then went out to acquaint the people on the streets with *Yeshua,* the Son of God, the One Who immerses with the Holy Spirit and with fire.

Joel, steadfastly pursuing his degree in Political Science, developed an almost superhuman schedule for himself, on his knees at his bedside for up to four or five hours a day, reading, studying, outlining the Bible, feeding his insatiable appetite for God.

David, pushing towards his degree in Psychology, attended his 7:00 and 8:00 o'clock classes, completed his assignments on campus, then rushed home to study his Bible for two or three hours, then "crash" until 5:00. That way he could join the others later, out on the streets, witnessing to whomever the Lord brought their way. Even with only about thirty thousand Jewish people in all of Cincinnati, and with only about three thousand of them on campus, the Lord kept leading them to unsaved Jewish people.

David and Joel both began amassing Bible translations and reference books, but mostly they studied the Bible.

Slowly, slowly, inexorably, we were turning, moving away from "Christian" labels and ways. We began using the Hebrew name *Yeshua,* instead of the anglicized-Greek *Jesus; Messiah,* instead of the Greek *Christ; syna-*

The Prayer Meeting

gogue, instead of *church; tree,* instead of *cross.* We were *immersed,* or *mikvahed,* instead of *baptized.* In place of Joanna, I became Yohanna Naomi – legally - an ironic twist from the Chernoffs in Canada, who anglicized their names in the mid-20s. By 1971, I was always singing, humming, or playing strong, vibrant, modern Israeli music from tapes, and urging our good-natured Joel to do the same. "This is what you should write!" I said. "This is the kind of music you should be composing!"

In June 1971, the heretofore staid and conservative HCAA, which customarily convened from city to city in large uptown, denominational-church buildings with velvet-cushioned pews, held its biennial conference at a Bible college in Oak Park, Michigan, a suburb of Detroit. It was still the only organization in the United States representing Jewish believers, and what would occur at this particular conference would impact the fledgling Messianic Movement for years to come. We were eagerly looking forward to see what the Lord would do differently.

The still unchartered YHCA members showed up in force - seventy youth, including Sandra Sheskin, an employee of the State Department in Washington, D.C.

We had already arrived and settled into our rooms in a dorm, when Joseph and Debbie Finkelstein, a young couple from Philadelphia, arrived. They pulled into the conference grounds with twenty-five of the most bizarre-appearing hippies we had ever seen - a band of "Jewish Jesus freaks" who had been meeting in their home, which the hippies appropriately and affectionately referred to as the "Fink Zoo." They all wore sweat-stained headbands, all clicked with beads and jingled with jewelry. Some came obviously in desperate need of deliverance from unclean spirits and from drugs. Undeniably, the Spirit of God was also among them.

Born a Jew...Die a Jew

Nevertheless, we were momentarily stunned. In comparison, our young people were plainly conservative. But these "freaks" from the Fink Zoo had a zeal for God, and it was love-at-first-sight between the two groups.

Until that meeting, HCAA members were happy to have fifty, sixty, maybe even a hundred people show up for their conferences. But that year, all the usual conferees brought their young new believers with them - masses of scruffy hippies right out of the drug culture. They streamed into the meeting room, rejoicing in the Lord, swinging their long, loose hair, barely held in place with head-bands, many dancing on bare feet, many still in long skirts or stained and ragged jeans. One girl brought her dog.

Appalled by the number and appearance of such characters, many older members voiced their objections, in no uncertain terms, that the newcomers were "loud, dirty, uneducated, unrefined, and ungroomed" - too unlike themselves. They feared, with good reason, from the sheer weight of numbers, that the newly saved hippies would eventually gain control of the Alliance, by voting their own members into office.

Finally, Arthur Glass, one of the older members of the Alliance, as well as Marty's old friend from Canada and the Carolinas, stood up and shouted over the hubbub: "What's the matter with us? For years we've been praying for a revival among our Jewish young people. It had to start with somebody somewhere, and HERE THEY ARE!" A scattered few of his age group joined him in welcoming the newcomers with smiles and handshakes, but others were soon stared down by their peers, who had realized with great misgivings that they were equalled in number by the new breed.

Marty moved among them, trying to convince some of the visibly shaken, older members of what we had

The Prayer Meeting

learned from personal experience, that many of these dropouts were, in reality, refined and educated, brilliant jewels in Messiah's crown. While he went about making peace, several Scriptures pounded into his mind about what God was actually doing in that place:

> *But God has chosen the world's foolish things to put to shame the learned; and God has chosen the weak in the world to shame the strong. God also has chosen the world's insignificant and despised people and nobodies in order to bring to nothing those who amount to something, so that nobody may boast in the presence of God.* 1 Corinthians 1:27-29

> *Did you never read, 'From the mouth of babes and nurslings Thou has perfected praise?'*
> Matthew 21:16

> *I praise Thee, Father, Lord of heaven and earth, because Thou hast concealed this from the learned and intelligent and hast revealed it to babes. Yes, Father, for thus it was pleasing in Thy presence.*
> Luke 10:21

From the first day of the conference, the Holy Spirit began performing miracles of God's grace, especially among the first-timers, who caught only rare snatches of sleep in order to fellowship throughout the night with our youth and with one another.

As Marty observed them, he silently thanked God for having blessed our children with religious schooling, with vacations spent with professing believers, and with homes always in stable Jewish communities, and, consequently, with being spared from most of the horrendous personal problems the other young people were facing.

In the middle of the week, during the official business meeting, Marty, who had been serving a two-year stint on the Executive Board since 1969, but who had never sought the limelight and never wanted it, was nominated and elected, in a very close election, as president of the HCAA for the customary two-year term. He accepted, reluctantly. Not really wanting the responsibility, and thinking maybe some votes which had been disallowed were for the man running against him, Marty suggested that they do a recount. As it happened, those votes were also for Marty, so he won by a slightly wider margin than was first believed. It was obvious that many of the Old-Guard Hebrew Christians were looking for a change.

Later, during the week, the young people raised the subject of Israel's victory in the 1967 Six Day War, especially the retaking of Jerusalem. They interpreted that victory as fulfillment of prophetic passages, specifically, the promise of Luke 21:24 and of Romans 11:25: *"Hardening in part has happened to Israel until the fullness of the Gentiles has come in,"* (NKJ). This verse, in particular, had taken on new and exciting meaning for them.

They no longer wanted to be known as Hebrew Christians. The term was awkward, they said. They had to spend too much time explaining what it meant. They had been calling themselves, "Jews who believe in Messiah Jesus," but that sounded too much like a definition. They wanted to be known simply as "Messianic Jews." Marty heartily agreed, and reinforced this simple title, because he recognized it as having come directly from the Lord.

During the late spring and summer that year, we spent long weekends in Philadelphia, fellowshipping with the

The Prayer Meeting

Finkelsteins and their brood, finding most of the coming-and-going hippies there eager to learn how to find new life in Messiah. The Finkelsteins both had Jewish backgrounds - Joe, Conservative, and Debbie, Orthodox. Their families still observed traditional Jewish customs, but Joe and Debbie had both been brought to *Yeshua* before their marriage in a traditionally Jewish wedding ceremony in a synagogue. Still maintaining a Jewish lifestyle, they emphasized to their new believers that they could accept *Yeshua* and still remain Jewish.

All during this time, Hope, whose heart was especially tender toward the hippies, with their multitude of unresolved problems, began spending her free time at home, and during the trips in the car between home and Philadelphia, searching the Scriptures for God's answers for her new friends.

Soon after we returned home, we noticed that our sons and some of their friends were wearing *yarmulkes* on their heads and big *Magan Davids* hanging down in front of their shirts like enormous Superman badges. They also began aggressively seeking friendships with unbelieving young Jewish people, and were eager to attend traditional synagogues on Friday nights, since we had, as yet, not started holding our own *Shabbat* services. Since Jewish young people seldom attended synagogue services, except on high holy days, when our boys showed up, they were asked why "such nice Jewish boys" were coming. "Why are you here? Where do you usually attend services?"

The questions always led to their being able to witness concerning Messiah. After awhile, however, the rabbis became suspicious of their motives, and said in effect, "You are welcome here, but you are not allowed to share about your faith any longer. If you do, we're going to ask you to leave."

Born a Jew...Die a Jew

Never disruptive, the boys' regular attendance, nevertheless, drew so many questions, that they were often asked to leave. Undaunted, they would attend somewhere else. Whenever they were suspected of witnessing too much, too often, they would be ushered out. It was becoming obvious that somewhere down the road we were going to have to start having our own *Shabbat* or Saturday morning services, Jewish but believing in *Yeshua*. That would be another major step that we and other Messianic Jewish pioneers were taking that would rock the religious world.

CHAPTER FIFTEEN

THE JOY OF MESSIANIC JUDAISM

With stammering lips and in aforeign language, He will speak to this people. Isaiah 28:11

1972: CINCINNATI, GRANTHAM

Early in 1972, as we began feeling less Christian and more intensely Jewish, Marty and I prayed about the holy days, and began to feel that, as Messianic Jews, we wanted to stop practicing the traditional church holidays, Christmas and Easter primarily, and to celebrate holy days that were Jewish. Of course, we still acknowledged the resurrection of the Messiah and His birth, even though it is not specifically commanded that we do so anywhere in the *Brit Hadashah*. However, we did see *Yeshua* in both these events, first as the slain Passover Lamb, and also as the Light of the World during *Hanukkah*. To our surprise, we discovered in the *Brit Hadashah* (John 10:22) that *Yeshua* Himself celebrated the festival of *Hanukkah* - confirmation that we were on the right path.

Our children agreed. We all wanted to celebrate Passover, to live it, to experience it as a congregation and as a family, not just demonstrate it for others. When the subject of Christmas came up, it gave Marty and me both some trouble. Since his youth, Marty had loved the excitement and friendliness of the Christmas season. Unable to participate as a child, he had envied his Christian neighbors' lighted trees, gala decorations, exchange of gif ts, and special holiday programs and other festivities.

I, too, had always loved Christmas. As a Hebrew Christian family, we had celebrated it in the traditional way, with cards and presents and special services, with our own tree, "stockings, hung by the chimney with care," and a big roast turkey. But we now strongly believed that we, as true Jews, should no longer celebrate Christmas that way. So, with a sigh, we put our Christmas ornaments away and chose to celebrate *Hanukkah* in its place. This Jewish holiday, known also as the "Feast of Lights" or "Feast of Dedication," commemorates Israel's victory over the Syrians in BC 165, the rededication of the Temple at Jerusalem, and the miracle oil in the Temple lamps that burned continuously for eight days. We decided to celebrate in a big way, lighting the special candles and giving gifts to each one of our children, one each night for the eight nights of Hanukkah, and we were satisfied.

In the spring, at the height of the revival going on in our own work, I suddenly felt the need to get away somewhere by myself, to fast and pray alone, and to renew my own perspective. I decided to travel throughout Florida, from Naples to Miami and Tampa. In all those cities, I saw "Jesus Houses," evidence that God was performing the same miracles everywhere, and I began to glimpse the scope of this enormous move of God among the youth of our nation. The Jesus House I visited in Miami was actually supported and run by young Jewish believers, and young Jewish people were flocking to it, giving their hearts to the Lord, being immersed in the Holy Spirit, speaking in tongues, and manifesting the love of God for one another and for whoever else came their way. After two months, I returned home to Cincinnati, renewed in spirit, mind and body.

Then, one morning, some concern about Marty's health and my own future slipped into my prayer time. When I committed it to the Lord, He spoke to me with comforting words:

> *Do you see a man skillful in his work? Before kings he will stand; he shall not stand before the undistinguished.*
> *Let not your heart envy sinners, but continue in the reverence [fear] of the Lord all the day; for surely there is a future and your hope will not be cut off.*
> Proverbs 22:29, 23:17

I was encouraged.

Joel, who had a slight stutter carried over from childhood, continued composing his contemporary songs - whenever he could drag himself away from his intense Bible study. Gradually, through his own vision and burden, and his retention of all the Hebrew and Yiddish music heard at home during his childhood and youth, he began creating something new - a contemporary, Messianic-Jewish sound, with a new feel to it. At the time, there was no other music like it.

Occasionally, he performed publicly with his friend Rick (Levi) Coghill, with Rick on steel guitar, and Joel on classical guitar, both singing Joel's powerful lyrics, taken mostly verbatim from the Scriptures.

Raised in the Episcopal church, Rick had been a well-known, popular, rebellious, heroin-addicted, rock musician since 1963, playing with a number of rock bands in the 60s, including the Lemon Pipers. When he came to know the Lord, he was delivered from addiction without suffering any withdrawal symptoms - a miracle of

God's love. His pastor sent him to "this other group where there are lots of young people." The "other group" turned out to be us.

Rick slid easily into Messianic music, with a strong desire to use his talents to help steer the worship of God back to its ancient, Jewish roots - back into soft, loving, worshipful adoration of God. Musically, he and Joel seemed to be meant for each other. Joel played all his songs for Rick, who joined right in on his guitar. They decided they liked the sound. Joel graduated from the University of Cincinnati in June, 1972, just before the YHCA conference. This conference was going to be a very special one. It had been decided by its leaders that it would be a totally Messianic Jewish youth conference and that it would be held for the second time at beautiful Messiah College, in Grantham, Pennsylvania. While those in attendance would probably not exceed one hundred, it was still the first such Messianic Jewish youth conference ever held. We were in great anticipation for what God was going to do at this meeting.

The weather, however, turned against the youth. In the wake of torrential rains, most of eastern Pennsylvania, especially the area around Harrisburg and Grantham, was flooded. The governor actually had to be rescued by helicopter from the second floor of the swamped governor's mansion.

Undaunted, our own young people showed up at our house with their backpacks on, and with high expectations, rearing to go. Marty had to say to them, "Sorry, kids. According to the radio, not only is the entire city of Harrisburg without water that's safe to drink, but all major highways between there and here are under water. We'd never make it."

Unconvinced, one of our young people spoke for the

others. "God is going to part those waters for us just like He did for Moses at the Red Sea!"

Was this young man prophesying? We couldn't be sure, but faith was high and the kids' faces bright with anticipation. We loaded our stuff and set out in caravan on what could have been the most foolish venture of our lives, singing and praising God as we saw the clouds part, then watched in awe as the flood waters receded before us to the other side of the sandbags all the way to Harrisburg, all the way through the city, and all the way up to Grantham.

Messiah College looked like a fortress surrounded by a moat, but there was one road in that was open, and we found it. Because the college had its own cistern, it was one of very few places in the whole of eastern Pennsylvania with plenty of crystal clear, pure drinking water. No doubt about it, God had ordained for us a miracle conference through the faith of a few young people who believed that He wanted them to be there.

About seventy youth attended, fifty-five more than in 1967, when the Youth Alliance first formed. All seventy of them expressed their desire to return to their Jewish heritage - the first stirrings of a Messianic-Jewish Youth Movement in our midst. Among them were Joe and Debbie Finkelstein, whose lives were destined to become enmeshed with ours.

God moved in a mighty way during the conference. There were constant, unscheduled prayer meetings and Bible studies in the dorms, young people accepting *Yeshua* as their Messiah, being delivered from drug addiction and their destructive life-styles, and entering into spontaneous prayer and praise that often lasted until dawn. When we finally got home, we agreed that none of us would ever be the same.

In the early fall, Marty and David were invited to go

Born a Jew...Die a Jew

with others from our youth group to the Ohio State University campus to talk to the students about their need for a Savior, and to acquaint them with Messianic Judaism. Some of the Ohio State football team members came out to listen. As expected, extremist Jewish radicals, notorious enemies of any Jew related in a positive way with *Yeshua,* and other radical groups showed up too. A few days later, when Darlene, the woman who had sponsored the meeting, was coming out of her house, some people drove by in a car and shot through the windows into her living room with a .22-caliber rifle. Evidently, it was one of the radical Jewish groups who attended the meetings, now sending a warning not to proclaim *Yeshua* as Lord any more on campus. That, however, didn't stop us.

David began working with some Orthodox students and other Jewish friends, both on and off campus, studying prophecy with them for hours on end, going back to the original Hebrew He soon displayed an urgent love and burden for all Jewish people, becoming more radically Jewish in his outlook than ever.

In mid-July 1973, Joel and Rick, and their friends Jerry Grubbs and Elliot Klayman strapped their guitars on over their backpacks, and took off to hitchhike and walk through Europe and on into Israel, playing informal concerts along the way, and, eventually, for the settlers in the Israeli kibbutzim and for people gathered on the beach at Tel Aviv.

They went on into Eastern Europe. In the mountains of Yugoslavia, they became exhausted from having walked more than twelve miles without catching a ride. Commercial busses would not stop for them. When they stopped in a deserted area to rest, Joel said, he actually became angry at God, reminding Him of His promise to watch over them on their journey. The Lord, in turn, re-

The Joy of Messianic Judaism

minded them that, because they feared the faces of men, every time they crossed over into communist territory, they had stopped witnessing. They experienced deep conviction and repented.

No sooner had they repented of their fearfulness than a stranger suddenly and mysteriously appeared by the side of the road. Surprised, and feeling foolish, not being able to communicate in words he could understand, they witnessed to him in sign and body language as best they could. The stranger went his way. Soon afterwards, somebody gave them a ride. When the driver let them out, however, they found themselves at the top of a 7,000-foot mountain in the middle of a thick cloud.

Exasperated, exhausted, and barely able to see their own feet in front of them, they lay down on their wet sleeping bags and wondered how they would get out of this seemingly impossible situation. Their return flight home would depart in just six days, from an airport in Greece, still hundreds of miles away. They reminded the Lord about it, just in case He had forgotten.

They were startled when a shot rang out. Or was it a shot? No, it was a loud backfire. Although they were still unable to see it, a car had pulled alongside the road and stopped not far from them. Because his vehicle had made such a loud noise, the driver had pulled off the road to see if anything had been damaged. He had stopped within a few feet of the boys.

Finding no damage, the driver was preparing to depart when the boys made themselves known. At the driver's invitation, they loaded their gear into his vehicle and climbed aboard. He drove them all the way to Belgrade, two hundred and fifty miles in the direction they needed to go, and the car never backfired again during that journey.

They arrived at the airport in Greece just in the nick

of time, and returned home transformed by the many miracles of protection and guidance God had performed for them. Joel soon left for Michigan to work, for the rest of the summer and early fall, at Chicago-based Peniel, a former Hebrew-Christian (Presbyterian) congregation, that was in the process of slowly transforming itself into a Messianic congregation and community center.

Not long after he left, we followed him, to spend our mid-August summer vacation at Peniel's wonderful camp grounds on the shores of Lake Michigan. We liked it there because Peniel's Jewish leadership thought it not sinful either to be or to act Jewish, nor to enjoy singing Hebraic songs. By then, our entire group had come to love Jewish music.

One day during a recreational period, we were sitting down on the beach, singing *Hava Nagila,* when two of our own young people jumped up, grabbed hands, and said, "Let's dance!" Immediately, others stood up to join them.

"Believers don't dance," we quickly reminded them. Marty and I were perhaps still more "assimilated" than we realized. We had been in believers' circles for a long time where any kind of dance was absolutely taboo.

The young people didn't seem to pay much attention. They danced innocently around in the sand as an expression of their joy. We finally shrugged and gave in, and many of the others from Chicago and Detroit joined them.

Later, at a meeting back home in Cincinnati, while our congregation was worshipping the Lord in song, we could actually feel the Spirit begin to move us through the music. Nothing out of the ordinary happened right then, but after the meeting, surrounded by such intense joy and energy, a number of our young people grabbed each others' hands and began dancing the *hora* around in a circle and singing *Hava Nagila.*

Marty and I exchanged glances. As leaders, what should we do? We hesitated, realizing that this could be the initial phase of some new way God was working among us. Above all, we did not want to quench the Spirit.

That was only the beginning. Our young people soon began dancing the *hora* after every service. Gradually, songs other than *Hava Nagila* were added. They danced before services as well, physically expressing the joy they could not otherwise contain. Dancing for joy before the Lord soon became an integral part of our worship. We had heard of "dancing in the spirit," when individuals danced more-or-less in ecstasy. But, as far as we knew, we had never heard of anyone dancing corporately before the Lord as an expression of love for God and as part of an actual worship service. We were learning a new thing.

In the midst of the blessing, the revival and the great joy we were experiencing, tragedy was about to strike. Within a period of six months, beginning in November, four different doctors would tell me, on four separate occasions, that Marty "might not live through the night." We were about to go through one of the greatest times of testing ever in our ministry; yet, ironically, we would also see some of the greatest miracles we had ever seen.

Chapter Sixteen

YESHUA – THE GREAT PHYSICIAN

Lift up your eyes, look round about and see! They are all gathering to come to you. As I live, says the Lord, you shall surely adorn yourself with them all as ornaments and fasten them on like a bride.

Isaiah 49:18

1972-1973: CINCINNATI

Early on November 4, 1972, Marty woke me up struggling for breath, and whispering, "Yohanna, Yohanna, I can't breathe. Take me to the hospital. I need oxygen."

Frantically, I woke up David, who was still living at home and attending the University of Cincinnati, and the two of us rushed Marty to the Emergency Room. The attendants took one look, enclosed him inside a cubicle, and started emergency treatment.

About midday, the doctor came out to us shaking his head, and said, "I'm sorry, but your husband has suffered a massive heart attack. I'm not sure he's going to live through the night."

I said, "What? Oh no, doctor, you must be mistaken. You must mean someone else's husband. My husband is here because he was having trouble breathing. It's his lungs, not his heart."

"Are you Mrs. Chernoff?" he asked.

"Yes."

"I'm not mistaken," he said. "Your husband is seriously ill. We don't know if he'll live through this."

The reception room began to whirl. How could this be? Marty was only fifty-two years old. All I could think of was that the accumulation of years and years of financial pressure, days and sleepless nights of intense prayer, and the constant stress of forging a pioneer movement, virtually alone, must have taken their toll on him. I looked around in shock. Everyone else in the room looked so despondent, so worried, so sad.

Then, out of the blue, the Lord spoke to me:

Do not mourn or weep ... Do not grieve, for the joy of the Lord is your strength. Nehemiah 8:10

I grabbed David's arm. "David," I said urgently, "we are not to grieve as the world grieves. We are to praise the Lord!"

Somewhat embarrassed, David, at first, hesitated, but then together we raised our hands and began praising the Lord out loud, to the astonishment of our small, grim audience.

"We praise You, God! We thank You, Lord, for what You are doing in there. We thank You that You are going to bring Marty through this crisis!" Our confidence was evidently contagious because the faces around us were not so despondent anymore.

Confident that we had prayed according to God's will and that He had heard us, we went home and called our people together for seven days of prayer and fasting for Marty's complete healing.

Within two weeks, he was home. The doctor who discharged him sent him home with a prescription medication called Coumadin, and with instructions on how to take it. Marty carefully followed the directions, but his legs and ankles soon began to swell, and he grew weaker day-by-day.

Several times I phoned the doctor, who sounded unconcerned, and considered it unnecessary for him to check on such unsettling side-effects. I tried not to worry.

But then one evening, as I was leaving to attend a Bible study, Marty reached out and said, "Yohanna, don't leave!"

"I have to go," I said. "I have to be there." And I left him. But, as soon as I sat down in my place, a voice said to my heart, "Go home to your husband. He is dying."

I jumped up and ran. By the time I got home, Marty was almost unconscious. I called an ambulance, and once again, we rushed him to the Emergency Room.

After examining him, the doctor appeared grim. He said, "Your husband has overdosed on Coumadin! His blood is so thin from it that he is already in heart failure. He may not live through the night."

Later that day, when Marty's condition had miraculously stabilized, the same doctor said, "You could sue for what has been done to your husband, and maybe you should." His prescription had been in error and the overmedication had thinned out his blood, stimulating heart failure.

For the next two days, we stayed in the hospital, hovering over Marty, praying without ceasing, while he continued in a coma, on the brink of death. During that time I decided not to sue. I did not want my husband to suffer another heart attack from being tied up in litigation.

After a few days, he finally came out of the coma, but he was exhausted from the ordeal and virtually bedridden.

Joel had moved to Chicago in early September to work at the Peniel Center. Hope, our very busy 15-year-old, was involved in all that was going on among the young believers in our congregation. David was preoccupied with balancing his study of the Word with completing his last year of college.

During this stressful time, he seriously appraised his father's desire for him to enter the ministry. When he realized that the "science of psychology" which he had chosen to study basically ignored the spiritual aspect of man's nature, he considered dropping it entirely and entering Moody Bible Institute's School of Jewish Studies. However, while praying for God's leading in this matter, the Lord impressed on his heart to stay right where he was, that he was in the center of God's will, and that what he was going to learn about this new Messianic Movement could not be taught in a seminary or Bible school.

In December 1972, when Joel returned home, Rick came to him with a proposition. A friend had suggested that they cut an album, and someone else was ready to finance the project. Rick believed they sounded good enough to go public. Joel agreed, since his stutter never interrupted his music, and he always sang smoothly. Their album was cut in three days in a local studio, and appropriately titled *Lamb I*, introducing *The Sacrifice Lamb*, which soon became a classic. *Lamb I* became an overnight success and was the top-rated album in Chicago for twelve straight weeks. Marty and I *kvelled* (rejoiced with big grins) all over the place.

Moishe Rosen, founder of "Jews For Jesus" in California, scheduled a Youth Crusade in the Arie Crown Theater in McCormick Place, a gigantic convention and exhibition center in Chicago's South Side, for February 1973, and invited Joel and Rick to Chicago to back him up musically during the Crusade. At first, Joel hesitated. Picturing himself stuttering before a crowd of five thousand, he asked for time to pray it through. "God," he

Yeshua – the Great Physician

said, "I won't do it unless You take away this stutter."

But God replied, "First you do it, then we'll talk about taking it away." So Joel quickly agreed to go.

Moishe had already sent flyers into the Jewish communities, announcing, "Moishe Rosen is coming!" Hundreds of people showed up, including the expected representatives of the Jewish Defence League.

Moishe's Youth Rally was apparently so successful, with so many Jewish youth responding to the Good News of the Messiah, that the JDL threatened to bomb the building. Protesters ganged up outside the doors. Undaunted, our young Messianic Jews from Cincinnati joined their Chicago friends and Moishe's crew in witnessing for *Yeshua*, not only to the Crusade attenders inside the auditorium, but also to the JDL protesters outside.

With this threatening and thrilling experience behind them, Joel and Rick both felt irresistibly drawn into full-time music ministry for *Yeshua*.

After their first spring concert in Cincinnati, the *Cincinnati Inquirer* (April 7, 1973) headlined, "Good and Godly music on Lamb's first album." From then on, the boys were inundated with requests to perform - in churches, on campuses, at coffee houses - more invitations than they could oblige, but they went wherever the Spirit led them, celebrating *Yeshua* the Messiah with their moving Messianic songs.

In the immediate afterglow of Lamb's successful concert, on a Sunday morning in April, four months after his hospitalization for heart problems, Marty got up and went into our bathroom to use the facilities without turning on the light. When he came out, I went in. As soon as I turned on the light, I stared in horror; the water in the toilet bowl was bright red with fresh blood.

Marty's life was being threatened again by some new medical emergency.

Chapter Seventeen

The New Wine

When the hour comes - and it is coming - will they recognize that a prophet has been among them?
In the time of their visitation, they shall stumble, says the Lord.   Ezekiel 33:33 and Jeremiah 8:12

1973-1975: Cincinnati, Dunedin, Philadelphia

When I saw the blood in the bowl, I gasped, not knowing what to do. Should I rush upstairs to alert Marty? Since he had gone up to have a quiet time with the Lord, I called his doctor instead.

"Get him to the hospital immediately!" he said.

Marty was getting ready to preach that morning, so I went in, sat down on the edge of the bed, and just quietly asked him, "Do you feel bad or anything?"

"No," he said. "I feel all right. Why?"

"I have to take you to the hospital," I said. "You were urinating blood."

Again, he was admitted immediately. The diagnosis: a malignant tumor on the kidney. Immediate surgery was called for. Even so, I felt a surge of faith that God was still in control.

On the way to the operating room, the surgeon said, "I cannot promise you, Mrs. Chernoff, that I will be able to remove the complete tumor. Because of the weakness of his heart from the heart attack and heart failure, I cannot even promise that he will come through the opera-tion." This was the third time I had heard these words concerning my husband.

"Oh yes, he will!" I said. "Twice last year, the Lord could have taken him if He had wanted to, either with the heart attack, or during the Cumadin crisis. He's not going to take him now! He'll be just fine!"

Where did that come from? I asked myself. But I already knew the answer. That kind of supernatural faith came only from the heart of God in response to the many, many prayers being raised for Marty and me, both by our faithful prayer group, who knew how to pray through, and our friends across the country. I myself had prayed through and had absolute certainty that my husband would not die.

After the surgery, the doctor scratched his head. "It's amazing," he said. "The tumor was so self-contained, it fell off in my hand. We removed the one kidney, but there was no sign of cancer anywhere else in the abdomen. It's quite amazing!"

It was another great healing in Marty's life. He could have died from cancer or even from kidney problems later in life. As we prayed, however, God did a miracle. Marty never had a problem with cancer again nor with his single kidney.

In spite of how amazingly the surgery went, we still had one more immediate hurdle to face. Every day, as we came to the hospital to visit Marty, instead of looking pale, he actually looked tanned and healthy. We just assumed that this was the hand of the Lord adding supernatural health to his supernatural healing. We were wrong.

One day, when we came to see our "tanned and healthy" Marty, we found him in quarantine. His color turned out not to be healthy at all. His skin and eyes had turned yellow, and he was diagnosed as having "in-

The New Wine

curable" serum hepatitis from contaminated blood transfusions he had received right after his heart attack. The quarantine was necessary because the disease was highly contagious. Once again I was told that he might not recover.

I called for emergency prayer. Even so, within a few weeks, Marty's weight was down to 98 pounds, and he looked like a concentration camp survivor.

Our little congregation prayed fervently for another miracle healing from our merciful Lord. After a few days, David and the elders decided that they should go in and lay hands on Marty for healing. They went to the hospital, put on smocks and masks, and entered the quarantine area, where they claimed and obeyed the Lord's command given through James:

> *Is anyone of you ill? Let him call the elders of the [congregation], and let them pray for him and in the name of the Lord anoint him with olive oil. The prayer of faith will restore the sick one, and the Lord will raise him up.* James 5:14-15

The men anointed Marty with the oil, and prayed. Then they left. Meanwhile, God gave me perfect assurance that Marty would come through this fourth crisis, as he already had the three previous ones within the last six months.

Within thirty-six hours, all trace of yellow in Marty's skin and eyes had disappeared, his appetite had returned and he was sitting up in bed, while the doctors tried to decide what had happened to him. Highly skilled doctors had diagnosed him as having serum hepatitis, but there was no sign of it now. Reputations were at stake, so the doctors decided that they must have been mistaken in their original diagnosis. Evidently, they said,

Marty had never had the disease in the first place. We knew better.

Marty's healing was quite dramatic, and David was profoundly impressed. It was his first experience in praying for supernatural healing when the prayer was followed by such an obvious miracle.

The morning after their prayer, during my quiet time, God had told me to bring Marty home, and by the time I arrived at the hospital, his color had returned to normal.

Marty's doctor was adamant, unconvinced of the miraculous healing. "He did not have serum hepatitis," he insisted.

"He was healed by God!" I said.

"He did not have it!" he insisted, signing the release, and attaching orders for a mandatory six-month recuperation period.

Back home, while still weak from the surgery and its complications, Marty voiced his need once again for David to help him in shepherding his flock. David agreed to pray about it.

Despite Marty's physical condition, the leaders of the fledgling Messianic Movement begged him to go down to Dunedin, Florida, for the 1973 June HCAA/YHCA conference and run for the presidency. If he did not, they feared, the Old Guard Hebrew Christians would crush this embryonic movement. Only Marty, they felt, could handle this crisis.

It was a difficult decision, but Marty believed that, for him, "There is no furlough while the war is going on." Normally he would have obeyed the doctor's orders and not subjected himself to the stress of travel and the pressure of a large conference and the battle it represented. But he had received, not only a supernatural

The New Wine

healing, but a supernatural restoration in his body, as well. And he felt up to making the trip.

So, two months after the surgery, we drove in a car caravan with a group of our young people and adults down to Dunedin, for what could prove to be the most critical conference for the Messianic Movement. We felt that recent opposition from the Old Guard Hebrew Christians confirmed that they were seeking to turn back the clock and to defeat the new move of God's Spirit. In Florida, we joined with the handful of other Messianic Jews whom we knew - from Chicago, Detroit, Philadelphia, and this time from Washington, D.C. and Baltimore, as well. We were thrilled to see how so many of them had blossomed and grown in their spiritual walk.

The conference was hosted by members of a Scottish Presbyterian church and their Jewish-Presbyterian pastor, who greeted us in the parking lot, welcoming us with their rendition of the Highland Fling, a Scottish folkdance in kilts with bagpipes and swords. What instant rapport we felt with them! When they stopped dancing, we started and were soon all dancing the *hora* in the parking lot. Right in the middle of the festivities, singing and dancing and praising God with all his might, was Martin Chernoff.

"Stop, Marty," I said. "Stop! Slow down! You need time to recuperate, like the doctor told you." He smiled and nodded his agreement but kept right on dancing.

What a perfect example of two cultures praising the Lord with their own indigenous dances! I thought, until I caught the undercurrent of criticism. Some of the Gentile believers and older Hebrew Christians were unhappy with dancing of the Messianic Jews and were, again, putting up the "middle wall of partition" between Jew and Gentile. Evidently, it was all right for Scottish Presbyterians to wear kilts, play bagpipes, and dance the fling, but wrong for Messianic Jews to dance the *hora,* or wear *yarmulkes* inside a church building. That realization caused us to decide privately, right then and there, that we would not have any more HCAA meetings in churches. We would find more neutral ground where we could freely express our Jewishness.

Regardless of the undercurrents, change was definitely in the air. The YHCA faction, formed in 1965 by those Finney would have called the "New Guard," and growing in numbers, was clamoring for the name of the entire organization to be changed from Hebrew Christian Alliance of America (HCAA) to Messianic Jewish Alliance of America (MJAA), in accordance with its new vision. This proposed name change became the focal issue that represented the differences between the two groups. The Old Guard Hebrew Christians continued to define their faith as a Jewish-flavored Christianity. They operated from within the church, they accommodated the church and they ultimately assimilated. The New Guard Messianic Jews saw their faith as true biblical Judaism, centered around *Yeshua* as the Messiah and wanted to stand on their own two feet and be as Jewish as the Lord led them to be.

The New Guard objected to worship services conducted in the old traditional Christian manner, which they felt was out of sync with Messianic Jewish worship. Unmoved by the old denominational hymns, they wanted the new, contemporary music instead. Marty, as president, encouraged the changes, and the revival fire swept on with the new music and praise songs. It could not be turned back.

A formal motion was made for the unprecedented change in name, but was defeated, even though it received 62 percent of the vote. A full two-thirds majority was needed to carry the motion. It was at this point that

The New Wine

a member of the Messianic New Guard stood up and insisted that a whole row or two had been skipped in the voting, and he wanted a recount. A member of the Old Guard cried out, "This is revolution!"

During the hubbub that followed, two Scriptures came to my mind:

> *When the hour comes - and it is coming - will they recognize that a prophet has been among them?*
> Ezekiel 33:33

> *In the time of their visitation, they shall stumble, says the Lord* Jeremiah 8:12

At this juncture, the HCAA and the entire Messianic Movement could have split asunder into two or more rival factions, had not Marty calmed the volatile situation. Respected by both sides, he proposed, with the wisdom of Solomon, that all those who wanted to be known as Messianic Jews, be recognized as such and all those who wanted to be known as Hebrew Christians be known by that name. He then challenged both sides to love and accept each other while waiting patiently to see what developed. He encouraged the New Guard Messianic Jews to be patient and to wait for the next national conference, which would be in two years, before bringing this issue up again. As a result, no recount was taken.

At the business meeting, held near the end of the week, Joel was elected president of the YHCA. Much to my chagrin, Marty, only recently out of the hospital after major surgery, was reelected by more than 80 percent of the vote into his second term as president of the HCAA. He was jubilant.

Born a Jew...Die a Jew

Later, in his "Message From the President," Marty wrote:

I have accepted the presidency of the Hebrew Christian Alliance of America for this second term with a sense of humility and deep responsibility... . We need unity and revival if we want the Hebrew Christian Alliance to "go on with God," for God is moving with or without us today. Let us determine we will work together, accepting differences, realizing that "God works in various times and in various ways" with His people Israel [Hebrews 1:1]... . In June, at the fifty-eighth National Conference of the Alliance held at Dunedin, Florida, we all clearly felt the differences of outlook between those Jewish Believers, young and old, who have been saved in the last six or seven years, and those of us who found our Messiah during the fullness of the Church Age (i.e., before 1967). We all sought to examine "new things springing up, " and to realize that God still works in various times in various ways to speak to His people Israel. ... We have much to give one another, and to learn and to share with one another, believing in the unity (though not necessarily the uniformity) of the Spirit.

David had graduated from the university before the convention. After we returned home, he had the entire summer before him. Like Joel the year before, David headed out with his own special friends, Jeff and Bruce Adler and Mike Rosenfarb, three other young Messianic Jewish young people from our congregation in Cincinnati, Ohio. For two months they backpacked through Europe and Israel on an unexpectedly spiritual journey, fraught with dangers and amazing miracles of protection all along the way.

The New Wine

As they were waiting for their flight to Israel from Athens, Greece, they felt impressed by the Lord to ask the hotel owners to allow them to stay in their rooms until 3:00 PM, as their plane did not leave until late that night. Usually this is not done, but to their surprise, the hotel allowed them to stay later. It might have just saved their lives. Because they relaxed in their hotel room for those few extra hours, they were spared from an attack by an Arab terrorist group called Black September. The group attacked the El Al office in Athens at the exact time David and his companions would have been there if the Lord had not led them to stay in their hotel later than usual.

David returned home from his trip, still unsure of what God wanted him to do with his life. He had been searching for a place where his Messianic ministry skills would fit in, but there were only a few embryonic Messianic organizations or congregations around at that time, and none of these seemed to be God's will for him at the time.

Meanwhile, Marty suggested he take over writing the monthly prayer-and-news letter that we had always maintained. "They're not hard to write," Marty said, "and you'll at least be making a couple-hundred a month salary writing it." Then Marty had a divine inspiration, a brand new idea, a radical concept: to incorporate an entirely original type of organization. It would be called Messianic Ministries, Inc. (MMI) and, through this new organization, David would be free to explore other avenues of ministry.

It was such a radical idea that they could not ask established churches to support it financially. They would have to see if funding for Jewish ministries would be forthcoming from individual believers. In Marty's mind, it was altogether possible that David would make a better fund-raiser than he had been. He had several advantages. The times were different; David was a college graduate; and the revival was on. So, perhaps this time around things would be different.

Marty asked, "What do you say, David?"

After much prayer and counsel David agreed. In preparation, he immediately assumed responsibility for the newsletter, continued with the congregation's successful campus ministry, accepted invitations to speak, and even took a job, substitute teaching, to subsidize the beginnings of the new ministry. He also assisted Marty in his ministry, wherever and whenever he could, gaining valuable firsthand knowledge and experience with the internal problems of ministry and how to deal with them.

Together, they took the plunge and incorporated MMI. The organization would work hand-in-glove with the congregation and would be under Marty's direct authority as its Executive Director and President. David became the Assistant Director of MMI. By then, he knew in his heart that he was called into full-time ministry.

While Marty was still recuperating, sometime late in 1973, our family and friends started sharing Friday night *Shabbat* meals to bind us together through that lovely Jewish traditional celebration. This was very controversial at the time. That anyone would consider having a Sabbath Service on Friday night was considered virtual heresy by many in the church. Indeed, many Jewish believers also considered it to be heresy. We found, however, that other Messianic Jews were beginning to experiment with the concept. We actually felt it was a prophetic and historic decision to begin having such *Shabbat* services.

David and some of the other Messianic Jewish youth in the congregation studied Jewish literature on how to

The New Wine

have a Sabbath service and began by following a somewhat traditional or liturgical type of service. Almost immediately we realized that the Holy Spirit was not leading us in that direction. Nothing in that traditional service attracted the young people, or any other Jewish people, for that matter. It didn't draw Jews to other synagogues, and we sensed that it wouldn't work for us. Messianic Judaism would develop its own personality, emulating neither Christian nor Jewish traditions.

We stopped striving, and changed our *Shabbat* services to one that focused on Davidic worship and praise and freedom in the spirit. From then on, young people were always in our house, either giving their hearts to the Lord, sleeping over, coming off drugs or just changing their life-styles, and bringing other young people in to find help, or just to share our Sabbath meal.

Early in 1974, David and some other Messianic youth from our synagogue organized the Messianic Jewish Movement Outreach (MJMO), our college-campus ministry. They set up tables on university campuses, passed out flyers, and brought in singing groups. Through this ministry they saw many extraordinary things happen, as they interacted with Jewish students. One incident in particular stood out to me:

In the spring, our campus workers, already good friends with the people in the Israeli Consulate, heard about a planned Palestine Liberation Organization (PLO) rally on the University of Cincinnati campus. Being very naive, we knew little about the PLO, and even less about terrorism; but we were disturbed that such people would be permitted to hold a big rally and banquet on campus. The Jewish campus organization, Hillel, was not planning to protest, so we decided to protest this gathering ourselves.

All the communist and socialist groups were organizing to support the PLO and come out in force. Four or five hundred were expected at the banquet. What could we do to demonstrate our outrage?

We asked the local Israeli Consulate for some Israeli flags. When he learned of the plan, the Israeli director for our area was shocked that a group of young Messianic Jewish youth wanted to demonstrate at a potentially hostile and dangerous gathering such as this. He agreed to help and gave the young people all the Israeli flags he had, about a dozen.

Before the rally began, I sneaked inside the auditorium and, armed with my tape recorder and camera, seated myself on the front row in the very center of the auditorium. I wanted to make the main speaker very nervous, sitting right under his nose, with my microphone pointing up at him.

Outside, twelve of our students lined up, six on a side, along the entrance into the banquet hall. Each one held up an Israeli flag, leaning the tops of the poles in, so that they touched at the top, like the rifles of an honor guard at a military wedding. Everyone who attended that banquet had to walk under the arch of Israeli flags. They did so with very puzzled expressions on their faces, expressions that quickly turned to anger when they realized that this was a Jewish protest (they did not understand the Messianic part yet).

Afterwards, a steady stream of Arab students came out to argue with our Messianic Jewish students, and they stayed out there talking for hours about Israel and about our Lord. When one young Arab girl realized that we were Jewish followers of *Yeshua,* she cried out in fear, "The end of the world is coming! The end of the world is here! The Jews now believe in Jesus! It's the end of the world!"

Joel had left for the summer to work at Peniel, leav-

The New Wine

ing his room and bed unoccupied. So, when Marty remarked to me, "This house is too empty," I interpreted it to mean that we had space enough to open our home to some of the young people who were getting saved. As a result, we began to open our home to young people on a more 24-hour-a-day, seven-day-a-week basis. And, again, many of the young people who continued to be drawn to our ministry developed clear leadership abilities and went on to become leaders in the Movement. It was as if God had developed a certain "apostolic flow" within the movement, as men and women went out from us to the revival. Many times it was not intentional, on our part, and we always recognized it as God's sovereign hand.

One young man who became a Messianic Jew during that time was BOB COHEN, a leader in the Students for a Democratic Society (SDS), a violent communist front group whose doctrine mandated revolution in America as the only way to change the social inconsistencies prevalent in our national economy. Bob had already been cited by the FBI as a communist leader in his high school. Regardless, I followed him around campus, as did some of our other young people, trying to talk to him about his need for the Lord. Bob showed absolutely no interest and, because of his heavy drug habit, soon dropped out of school. Still, I wrote him letters and kept track of him. In the end, the persistent love of the Lord overcame his rebellion, and he finally surrendered his life to the Messiah. Today, he is a full-time Messianic Rabbi serving the Lord.

BOB WINER was another. A premed student at the Ohio State University Medical School, Bob became acquainted with our young people, gave his heart to the Lord, and became a leader in his own right, compiling the history of the Messianic Jewish Alliance of America in his book, *The Calling*.

MARK DAYAN also became a believer during this time, and is now a nationally-recognized song and worship leader.

MARGO LUNKEN (now Yesner), former hippie and ex-debutante, gave her heart to the Lord, moved in with us, and became a very valuable laborer in our ministry.

One of the students I tracked down on campus was JOYCE REICHMAN, an 18-year-old Jewish girl from New York City. A card-carrying communist like Bob Cohen, Joyce was very vocal in her support of the Chicago Seven and the Black Panthers. Intent on formenting revolution on campus, she organized a division of the SDS for women. The news media took pictures of her with two men wearing black leather jackets and black berets, pulling down an American flag and trying to raise a Vietcong flag in its place at the top of the flagpole. She was arrested at Fountain Square opposite City Hall, and her picture appeared on the front page of the *Cincinnati Inquirer*. That episode ended her college career, and forced her to return home to New York.

For thirteen months thereafter, I carried the newspaper article covering her arrest in my purse, praying for her to become a believer. Eventually, she returned to Cincinnati, where God led her to a position as secretary to ELLIOT KLAYMAN, a handsome, young, radical, Jewish lawyer with masters degrees from both the University of Cincinnati and Harvard.

Elliot had recently become a believer himself. Several months after he first introduced Joyce to *Yeshua*, she had a wonderful, salvation experience - just thirteen months after I set myself to pray for her. Before they married, they looked us up, and both became active members of our congregation.

The New Wine

WHAT A WONDERFUL HARVEST! We are grateful to the Lord.

Later that same summer, it seemed to us that our divine appointment in Cincinnati was drawing to a close. God had taught us much during our more than twenty years in the relatively "quiet waters" of Cincinnati. Marty's vision of Messianic Judaism had been birthed there. God had shown us some key principles for establishing and running an independent Messianic synagogue, everything from government to liturgy to praise and worship. And a whole host of young people had been redeemed and were on their way to becoming leaders in the Movement, a gift from the sovereign hand of God.

We felt sure now that the Lord had something else for us. Every time we prayed about whether the Lord was indeed leading us out of the city, Marty received the same word from the Lord:

> *Do not despise this small beginning.*
> Zechariah 4:10, TLB

> *Do you not say, Four months more and the harvest will be here? Look, I tell you; raise your eyes and look at the fields, how they are white for harvest.*
> John 4:35

But if we had finished our work in Cincinnati, what were we to do now?

Marty loved people, and people loved him. Always warmhearted and friendly, even playful at times, he had a natural gift for attracting people to himself. He loved them, enjoying nothing more than sitting and talking with a group of them. He set an example of friendliness that most found hard to emulate, yet he never came off as condescending. Always available for counseling those in the movement, especially other Messianic rabbis and leaders, he also asked for opinions from our daughter Hope, as well as from our sons.

At the same time, Marty was a tough pioneer and, as with most pioneers, he experienced opposition against his convictions, especially as to which direction God was leading us. Marty seldom answered his detractors, and never defended his course of action publicly. He had taken as his guideline the famous words of Oswald Smith in Toronto: "No defense and no offense." For years, that was the motto of our ministry. He wasn't afraid to make a radical move now.

We had heard many reports of Jewish people in the large metropolises, Messianic Jews who were hungry to know the Lord intimately, but were not willing to commit to a traditional church. We now felt the call to "launch out into the deep," somewhere where Marty could reach those "lost sheep of the House of Israel." God encouraged him from the Word:

> *[Yeshua] ... was moved with compassion for them, because they were like sheep not having a shepherd.*
> Matthew 9:30

During our times of beseeching God for guidance in finances and other matters of concern, and in our intercession for the unsaved, our prayers always seemed directed toward the multitudes of Jewish youth in the big, overcrowded cities. Many were making professions of faith, then losing their way. They wandered around, rejected by family and old friends, but not able to tie in with a Christian group that could or would disciple them, thereby grounding them firmly in the faith. Maybe we, as Messianic Jews, were not doing everything we

The New Wine

could to reach them and keep them grounded in the Word of God.

We felt now that God was leading us to one of the major Jewish population centers of the country. But which one? We confided only in our children, and together we prayed about this matter for some time privately, feeling strongly that, if we were going to make a change at all, the time had come.

Afraid that the news would cause confusion, misunderstandings, and hurt feelings within the Cincinnati congregation, we postponed telling anyone else until we could find a suitable replacement for Marty. Quietly and diligently we searched for just the right person - God's choice for the position.

This proved to be no easy task. Jewish workers were accustomed to working for a salary from an established organization, and none of the potential candidates had ever heard of a self-supporting Messianic congregation and found the concept to be intimidating.

Meanwhile, Joel, our recently-elected president of the YMJA, held a Lamb concert in Philadelphia, and stayed with the Finkelsteins. While there, he shared our quest with Joe and Debbie. As a result, Joe phoned Marty in November to ask if he would be willing to become the Messianic rabbi in Philadelphia, to pastor the wild and wonderful "Fink Zoo" fellowship, and try to mold them into a congregation.

After his call, we studied the map. Philadelphia, the City of Brotherly Love, sat right in the middle of four million Jews, all within two hours driving time of the city. There were four hundred thousand Jews within the city proper of Philadelphia. Many of those four million Jews, we were sure, needed to know their Messiah.

In December, we visited Philadelphia to discuss the situation with the Finkelsteins and their thirty regulars, which included a lively twelve-member, newly-formed group calling themselves, "The Messianic Singers." They were wonderful. Joe seemed eager to turn the work he had started entirely over to Marty, so that he could focus his time and energy on the music group.

Prayer was our natural imperative. All the details of any venture must first be conceived in prayer, then brought to birth through prayer. After much prayer and waiting upon the Lord, we were soon convinced that it was His will for us to make the move.

To the ... [congregation] in Philadelphia ... See, I have provided an opened door in front of you, one which no one is able to close; because, while possessing little strength, you have observed My word and have not renounced My name. Revelation 3:7-8

We eventually contacted Rachmiel Frydland, Warsaw ghetto survivor, Bible scholar, and Messianic Jewish believer, well-known around the world, but based in Toronto, a man greatly loved and revered by all who knew him, and asked him to pray about taking charge of our existing local congregation. Rachmiel agreed almost instantly, feeling sure it was God's will for him to move to Cincinnati. He, his wife Estelle, and their four beautiful children made preparations to move.

We accepted his avowal of confidence as God's confirmation for us to move on to Philadelphia. But where in Philadelphia? Should we move to the northeast section of the city where the majority of the Jewish people lived? Or should we move to the west side of town, where most of the political and social power seemed to be concentrated? We were unsure. "Lord," we prayed, "You know we don't have much money, but we're going to need a big house with at least four bedrooms."

The New Wine

Within days of that prayer, Joe sold us their very spacious brick home with four bedrooms and room to expand. It was on lovely, shady Sherwood Drive in Greenhill Farms. It had been used for Messianic ministry as the "Fink Zoo" for a number of years, and they wanted ministry in that home to continue.

Meanwhile, David, as Marty's assistant, flew up to Philadelphia three times to help prepare the way for us. First, he and Joe hired a reputable lawyer to draw up a charter and constitution for our new congregation. Then, with the help of Debbie, he successfully established an active and independent branch of the Messianic Jewish Movement (MJM) on the University of Pennsylvania campus as well as Temple University.

In October, ten months before we arrived, the new MJM members were allotted half of the front page in *The Philadelphia Inquirer's* Section B, because of their creative promotion, the "Dry Bones Parade." According to the article that accompanied three large photographs:

> *The message that eight members of the Messianic Jewish Movement were pushing at the University of Pennsylvania Thursday was straight from the Old Testament, but their methods were Madison Avenue. Their faces covered with white make-up and their bodies draped in long robes, they marched silently across campus carrying a sack of dry bones. The make-up and robes were to make them look like Old Testament prophets. The bones refer to a biblical prediction that the Hebrews, scattered like dead bones, would come together again and live. The point was to publicize their showing of a movie "Dry Bones" on campus Sunday.*

With some of the other members wearing sweat shirts

Born a Jew...Die a Jew

with "Messianic Jewish Movement" emblazoned across the front, they caused a near riot. The community knew without question that the Messianic Jews had arrived.

We announced to the members of *Beth* Messiah, our congregation in Cincinnati, our intentions to move to Philadelphia and that Rachmiel Frydland had agreed to become the new Messianic rabbi of the congregation. At first some of the members were shocked and upset, but they respected Rachmiel and welcomed him, when he and his family moved to Cincinnati.

In June 1975, the HCAA/YHCA joint Biennial Conference was again held at Messiah College in Grantham. This meeting proved to be another watershed for the Movement, for a number of reasons: It was the first time a conference attracted twice as many of the New Guard Messianic Jews as had attended the 1973 conference in Dunedin - about eight hundred altogether, comprising almost 90 percent of the conferees. Many came from a dozen or more brand new Messianic congregations, including a few Messianic Jewish visitors from England and France. By sheer weight of numbers, they easily outnumbered the Old Guard Hebrew Christians.

At the center of this "changing of the guard" stood Martin Chernoff, always a consistent, steadying influence, having served as president of the HCAA for four years.

For the second time, the motion was made to change the name of the organization to the Messianic Jewish Alliance of America (MJAA). The vote was overwhelmingly in favor, no doubt due to the fact that many conferees were just over twenty years of age, and all the younger generation were in favor of the change. According to historian David Rausch, in his *Messianic Judaism,* "The name change ... signified far more than a semantical expression - it represented an evolution in the thought

The New Wine

processes and religious and philosophical outlook toward a more fervent expression of Jewish identity."

Joe Finkelstein succeeded Marty as MJAA president, and David was elected president of the YMJA. Soon, hundreds of young Messianic Jews became actively involved in the Movement. Unfortunately, many of the Old Guard were offended by the changes that were coming so swiftly and never again attended the conferences.

The conference at Messiah College proved so successful that it was decided to have our future conferences there. When that one was over, we returned home to Cincinnati to get ready for the move to Philadelphia.

A few members of our "extended family" in Cincinnati, many of them saved under our ministry, decided to go with us. On July 15, 1975, Marty, Joel, David, Hope and I moved to Philadelphia. Those who also moved from Ohio a month later, to be with us, were Margo Lunken (now Yesner), Bob Winer, Helen Weiner (now Wilson), Marlene Gurewitz (now Rosenberg), Rick Coghill, Mark Dayan, Dick Weidus, and Barry Simon.

Moving was a tremendous leap of faith, especially for Marty, coming just three years after his heart attack, but we were willing to give up everything to start over, having no idea of where it would lead, and with no guaranteed financial backing. We had come this far by faith, and we were sure that God would not forsake us now.

The Messianic Jews in Philadelphia welcomed us with the offer of a generous and adequate salary that would amply cover all our living expenses. One member spoke for them all, "Rabbis in traditional synagogues get nice salaries, so our Messianic rabbi is going to get one too!" I watched Marty's face, knowing he would have been happy with much less. He did not refuse. The money was there, they wanted us to have it, and we were thankful. All our lives we struggled with finances, but when we went entirely independent, with no backup plan, remaining true to the vision God had given us, that act began a period of financial success that we had never experienced before. The pressure was off.

With so much confirmation coming from all sides - the precise timing and all the particulars - we fully expected to steal quietly into town. We would set up housekeeping, incorporate a new congregation, print our offbeat provocative tracts, brochures and books, pay our bills, win new people to salvation in the Lord, and live at peace with our new neighbors. Quietly and unassumingly, we moved in, simply the vanguard of a new movement. Nobody would hassle us, and all would be peaceful. Boy, were we wrong about that!

PART III

Chapter Eighteen

Opposition

I am sending you to the children of Israel ...
As for you, son of man, be not afraid of them, nor afraid of their words; though briars and thorns are all around you and you dwell among scorpions, do not fear their words nor be dismayed at their looks. Ezekiel 2:3,6

1975-1979: Philadelphia

The move to Philadelphia was an exciting step for us. Once there, we entered a new phase of our ministry, and a number of changes took place. Suddenly, we were in one of the largest Jewish communities in the world; the spotlight was upon us; and we found ourselves on the front lines spiritually, the cutting edge of what God was doing in Messianic Judaism. We also found that the principles we learned from the early years of the Movement, from 1970 to 1975, we were now able to implement and develop.

The number of former hippies meeting regularly in the Finkelsteins' living room was, by then, up to about 30-35, most of them already faithful in tithing. That, in itself, relieved a great deal of pressure on us as a family. Having been very loosely organized up to that point, however, all of them had trouble adjusting to strong leadership - which we had come to believe was both biblical and vital for congregational success.

Traditional congregational structure at this time was

very denominational. The congregation voted in the elders, and either the elders or the congregation, in turn, voted in the pastor. Therefore, the pastor was under everyone, at the bottom of the ladder, basically an employee of the congregation.

Marty had seen traditional, congregational structures in the past, with elections, congregational business meetings, and all the rest; but the resulting factions, splits, and other divisive problems encountered led him to believe that the pastoral system, where the pastor, or Messianic rabbi, was basically in charge with appointed elders working under him, was the one that worked best - at least when the Messianic rabbi or pastor is truly appointed by God. In the traditional setup, as well, if the spiritual leader of a congregation stepped out of line (or on someone's toes, God forbid), he could be fired. Obviously, it would be very difficult, under those circumstances, for true leaders to develop. No one could have fired Moses or Isaiah or King David or Peter or Rabbi Shaul!

Just as Moses received a pattern from God for the Tabernacle (Exodus 25:9,40), and King David received a pattern from the Lord for the Temple worship and building (1 Chronicles 28:11-12), so the Lord gave to us a "new" pattern, not only for congregational worship, but for congregational government, as well. It is interesting to note that this pattern of leadership is now quite common in both Messianic Judaism and Gentile Christianity today. However, for us, at the time, it was brand new and another step of faith we had to take in order to operate in leadership the way we knew God wanted.

In Philadelphia, we started with a nucleus of believers who agreed to support both their synagogue and their rabbi by the biblical system of tithing, as laid down in the Torah. Together, we formed an independent, autono-

Opposition

mous congregation, which we simply named *"Beth Yeshua"* (House of Salvation). This Messianic synagogue would be supported solely by the tithes and offerings of its members.

At the start, God showed us to go slow in appointing elders, until we were stabilized and sure that each had a Messianic vision, and not just a desire for position. We started with one rabbi and two elders who made most of the decisions: Marty, Messianic rabbi and head of the congregation; Joe Finkelstein, elder and MJAA president; and David, elder and recently-elected YMJA president.

Despite his healing, Marty had ongoing problems with his health. While he was a walking miracle, he had to be careful. In reality, he was operating with only half of a heart, as a result of his heart attack. Consequently, in the MJAA, after carrying the responsibility and burden of this new Messianic Movement for more than eight years, he began to move into more of an advisory capacity and let some of the new Messianic Jewish leaders begin to carry the vision. He remained the guiding force behind the Alliance, as well as our new Messianic synagogue in Philadelphia. He was a prayer warrior, a visionary and a wise counselor, pastoring and ministering the Word, soul-winning and practicing deliverance Ministry - a true revivalist-intercessor.

Besides being able to implement in Philadelphia all the principles of Messianic Judaism we had learned in Cincinnati, we felt it was time for us to branch out in other areas. And many more issues needed to be settled. One of the main issues we grappled with, at the Messianic conferences and at home, was what kind and how much, if any, rabbinic liturgy we should institute. Some of the members preferred a traditionally Orthodox-type service, with much Hebrew, liturgy, a Torah scroll and prayer books.

Born a Jew...Die a Jew

We had already made and forsaken a move in that direction. Marty had been brought up in a strict Orthodox Jewish home, so, from the start, he opted for the structure to be kept loose, with only a certain limited amount of liturgy and Hebrew. There would be no Torah scroll at the beginning of our ministry, which was often carried around the synagogue during every service with congregants reaching out to touch or kiss it. Marty was concerned, with good reason, that people tended to worship the Torah, turning their eyes and attention away from the Lord and His written Word, to the physical scroll itself. Also, he was concerned that people would get wrapped up in a love for the liturgy and prayers and literally make the same mistake as the Pharisees did in the days when *Yeshua* was upon the earth, focusing on man-made traditions rather than the living Word of God.

Marty felt that our Jewish people had a hunger for a personal experience with God and the things of the Spirit. Many Jewish people had left synagogues because of the dryness, formalism and dead liturgy. We believed that this move of the Holy Spirit could not be improved by *"the [religious] works of the flesh"* (Galatians 3:3), man-made traditions, and principles that all resulted in a type of denominationalism. To us, unity in the spirit and cohesiveness far outweighed any other aspect that might be lacking. *Shabbat* was still *Shabbat,* and we would keep our Friday night services as the Lord led us, not simply by the dictates of tradition.

We were more interested in getting our Jewish people saved than in preserving an ideal of traditional Jewish liturgy, which only a handful of very religious Jews followed anyway. Most of the Jewish community, in Israel and throughout the world, have already rejected Orthodox Judaism for themselves. They are not interested in

Opposition

a life full of strict religious observances. Our feelings on this issue echo what the first-century Messianic Jewish *shaliach* (apostle) declared at the Jerusalem Council:

> *Now then, why be a trial to God by placing a yoke on the neck of the disciples, which neither our fathers nor we were able to carry?* Acts 15:10

Yeshua also dealt with this issue. When asked why His disciples transgressed the tradition of the elders, He responded:

> *Why do you transgress the command of God through your tradition? ... So you have nullified the Word of God through your tradition.* Matthew 15:3, 6

This controversy reminded us of the historic controversy between Theodore Herzl and the well-known philosopher and cultural Zionist, Ahad Ha-Arn, about 1900 A.D.. To Ha-Arn, the ingathering of the exiles to Israel was of little importance. He did not concern himself with the plight of the Jews of *Diaspora.* His concern was saving traditional Judaism. He said, "We are not concerned with saving Jews but Judaism."

Herzl was concerned with saving Jews from the holocaust, which he foresaw, and in establishing their Land. He said, "Judaism without Jews? We know you, you beautiful mask - go join the Spiritualists!" He was concerned with the masses.

Herzl saw "cultural Zionism" as a trend that would only obstruct the Zionist effort to rescue large masses of Jewish people. Marty, too, felt that if some believers in the Messianic Movement turned aside to save dead traditionalism and liturgy, it would freeze out the masses of Jewish people hungering for the pure Word of God and the Holy Spirit. He said, "Messianic Judaism should concern itself in proclaiming salvation to the masses of Jewish people and turning them to their Messiah. PUSH FOR REVIVAL! Messianic Judaism will develop its own traditions."

Some called Marty "too much of a pragmatist," but even today we need to think through the principles of Spiritual Zionism (Messianic Judaism) to make sure we are not sacrificing apparently Spirit-led services in order to copy "traditional" Judaism and liturgy, which has frozen out hungry souls for hundreds of years.

In October of 1976, we received another unexpected blessing from the Lord. A Messianic Jewish woman whose young daughter needed to give up her son for adoption came to us and asked if any of our Messianic couples might like to adopt him. I shocked my family by walking into the house one evening with this beautiful, four-month-old Jewish baby boy. He stayed with us for six months, then Joe and Debbie Finkelstein were led of the Lord to adopt him. Soon "Avi Finkelstein" became a member, not only of the Finkelstein household, but of ours, as well. One Bible teacher said that adopted children are twice blessed by God, and I have found this to be true. This little boy became a great blessing to us all.

In our fledgling congregation, it took us almost two full years to develop the strong core group necessary for spiritual growth. Still, we were growing, and in 1975, we moved *Beth Yeshua*'s services from our house to the Marriott Hotel, then quickly outgrew even those facilities, moving again, in 1978, to the Holiday Inn.

Meanwhile in Cincinnati, *Beth Messiah* was once again in need of a Messianic rabbi. Marty understood from the Lord that he was to raise up and train someone else from our group in Philadelphia to go, someone with a strong pastoral calling. A young Messianic Jewish believer

Opposition

named Michael Wolf was Marty's choice. A staunch believer since 1972, Michael, with his wife, Rachel, gladly moved to Cincinnati in 1977 and quickly became their beloved and successful rabbi.

Had I been harboring even fleeting doubts that we were in God's will, they vanished completely that summer at the close of a *Kol Simcha* ("Sound of Joy") concert at the 1977 MJAA Conference in Grantham. As I stood alone in the bleachers, the Lord granted me one of my few visions. In it, I was caught up with *Kol Simcha* into a pink cloud, when a voice spoke to my inner man: **"Creative forces for Messianic Judaism shall flow forth from Philadelphia."** Not completely understanding what this meant, I was, nevertheless, overwhelmed with joy.

Thus mightily encouraged, in the fall of 1977, we embarked on another huge development for our fledgling ministry and the Movement. We opened *Chalutzim* (Pioneers) *Day School,* very possibly the first congregation-sponsored Messianic academy in the Movement at the time.

Chalutzim was geared specifically towards the children of our own Messianic Jewish families, with Linda Krause (now Linda Brown) as our founding principal and teacher. Supporting an academic core curriculum for only a few lower grades, the school also offered courses in Jewish history, Hebrew, modern Zionism, and spiritual discipleship from a Messianic Jewish perspective.

Since we had no congregational building at first, the school met in our homes, but as soon as the Jewish community found out about it, they reported us to the Zoning Board to close us down. It was, they said, "illegal" to conduct school in a home. Eventually, we were able to continue legally by using the nursery of one of the local churches, but we were praying fervently for our own building.

Born a Jew...Die a Jew

There were still only a couple dozen Messianic synagogues in existence, most of them in rented facilities. Buying a building of our own seemed like an impossible dream. By 1977-78, however, we had grown so fast that we were forced to begin searching for our own building.

It was while we were looking for a permanent home that the first of a series of articles appeared in the local *Main Line Jewish Exponent* newspaper. It was entitled "Messianic Menace on the Main Line." The article had numerous pictures of smiling young people (supposedly ours, but actually "Jesus freaks" from California), carrying signs proclaiming, "Jesus, the Name You Can Trust."

One outraged local rabbi was quoted in the article as saying, "These people are crazy. They exhibit a tremendous ignorance of Judaism. A few of them have even tried to convert me!"

Quoted from another rabbi was the warning, "The portrayal of themselves as authentic Jews is insidious, historically false and misleading . ... They give a totally Christological interpretation of Jewish history, and I reject it. I don't see any difference between them and the early Church Fathers. The only difference may be a subtle organizational and not theological one. That's why they are so dangerous."

The article ended with the words, "Continued next week."

The next article in the series was similar, and this continued, until the publication of the weekly articles put a surprising amount of pressure on us. We had never faced this kind of organized persecution. This "campaign" put us at odds with the very Jewish community that had brought us to Philadelphia in the first place. These were the people with whom we were trying to share our faith in *Yeshua*.

Opposition

Despite the pressure the articles put on us in the community, we were glad that *Yeshua's* name was being broadcast. We could identify with Rabbi Sha'ul who rejoiced that, from motives pure or impure, *Yeshua* was being proclaimed (Philippians 1:15-18). We even agreed with P.T. Barnum, who said, "I don't care what negative things are said about me, as long as they spell my name right." We took the attitude that God was using our situation to spread knowledge of *Yeshua* the Messiah and Messianic Judaism as well, even if it was from a negative perspective.

Until that time we had also not been bothered by groups of "anti-Messianic" people which developed within movements formed across the country to combat cults and reprogram their rescued "victims." Now, feisty, radical young Jews, calling themselves "anti-missionaries," were forming groups on college campuses and in Jewish communities, groups dedicated to persecuting Messianic Jews, often in very unscrupulous ways. To them the end justified the means.

Incensed and still infuriated by the Dry Bones Parade in 1974 and our successful campus ministry, by the fall of 1978, the opposition was ready for us. Every time our young people went onto the local campuses to set up tables where the students could help themselves to our materials - brochures, Jewish New Testaments, tracts on such subjects as *"Was Jesus a Jewish Messiah?"* and the like - the waiting anti-missionaries worked with a vengeance. Some tried to monopolize our time and attention so that we could talk to only a very few genuine inquirers.

"So, what kind of literature do you have?" the anti-missionaries asked, not really wanting to know.

"What is all this? What are you trying to prove? There's no such person as Jesus, the Jewish Messiah!"

Born a Jew...Die a Jew

"You're not Jews. You're Christians, masquerading as Jews. You're trouble makers."

"Why are you trying to confuse these poor students? They have enough on their minds already."

"This stuff is all lies, and you know it!"

Others intercepted all Jewish students who even looked like they might be interested, by intimidating and harassing them, even blocking their way to our tables.

At the same time, the organized Jewish community leaders, feeling threatened by our presence, as tiny as we were, began to oppose us. Labeling us "missionaries," they moved against us by writing anti-Messianic articles for local newspapers, in which they branded us "a cult of Christian missionaries pretending to be Jews, but funded by the Church." Many such lies were published, warning the entire Jewish community about us. They wielded such sudden and powerful influence locally that we were taken completely by surprise.

We received a report that a strategy of harassment and persecution against us from the Jewish community was being planned in secret meetings. And, because we were one of the larger Messianic congregations at that time, they were seeking ways to shut us down. If they succeeded, they would then know how to proceed in their plans to attack and shut down other Messianic congregations, most of them smaller than ours and, like us, without a building of their own.

What should we do? After praying about it, we felt that we should do nothing. We had always believed that where there is revival, we shouldn't force it. So, we also could not stop to defend ourselves either. We had to just continue following the leading of the Holy Spirit.

As we determined to do so, Jewish souls were coming into the Kingdom, many young believers were being discipled, the campus ministry was going strong,

Opposition

Bible-study groups and prayer groups were gaining strength and numbers, and both the congregation and the Movement were growing.

The Holy Spirit was giving us many new songs, some in Hebrew. God was leading us to witness of the Messiah by any and every means, and we just needed to keep on keeping on. That was to prove a challenge.

City Line Avenue, right around the corner from us, was so named because it marks the dividing line between the middle-class city proper and the exclusive Main Line suburb of Montgomery County, encompassing the late Grace Kelly's family home, the Dupont estates, Chestnut Hill, Mt. Airy, Bryn Mawr College, and other famous sites of Philadelphia, and very wealthy Jewish neighborhoods. When the Jewish community caught wind of the fact that we were looking for a building in that area, the persecution began in earnest. A synagogue meant permanence, credibility and strength, and they could not permit it.

On our side of City Line, middle-class Overbrook Park stretches through street after street of Philadelphia's famous, identical, stone row-houses, just twenty minutes from downtown on the bus line. It is a unique community of low-cost housing where the nucleus of our people lived at the time. When many of our members moved to Philadelphia, it was to Overbrook Park. Eventually, by 1978, we had the beginnings of a unique Messianic community right in the heart of the Jewish community. We did not exactly plan it to happen, but it was God's pattern for us.

Marty had been shown by the Lord, in the mid-70s, that these were the Last Days and that believers should strive to live together in community, if possible. In Cincinnati, we had always lived close to other Messianic believers.

Messianic community life, very similar to the community life found in Jerusalem in the first century (Acts 2:42-47), would soon become one of the foundations and hallmarks of our synagogue. I have had many Messianic rabbis say to me that they wished they could have had such a wonderful community, where believers lived near each other, could walk to services, and could fellowship with each other almost daily. Community life means a close relationship with one another, something beyond just a once-a-week congregation. The concept is biblical, spiritual and much needed today in both Messianic Judaism and Gentile Christianity.

While our Messianic community was growing in the late 70s, we still had a number of members who lived outside of the community, in various parts of the city. Consequently, we wanted to purchase a building which would be centrally located. We found one for sale on Latches Lane, just one block over into the Main Line section. It was at most a five- or ten-minute drive from the center of Overbrook Park, and we considered it to be a prize, an enormous, old, deserted stone mansion on four neglected acres.

For years, nobody had wanted to tackle the extensive restoration needed to make the house livable. So it was very reasonably priced. It was also already zoned for our purposes. We felt that we could renovate the building and add an auditorium and that the four acres could be landscaped into a peaceful setting for celebrations, retreats, and possibly even a community center.

We committed the place to the Lord in prayer. When we believed we had His go-ahead, we made a reasonable offer for the property, and, to our great joy, our bid was accepted. Then, however, all "hell" broke loose. Once again, the Jewish community organized against us. Details of all pending real-estate transactions in the suburban Philadelphia area are regularly published in

Opposition

the local newspapers, and we had made the fatal error of submitting our bid in the name of *Congregation Beth Yeshua.*

The Jewish Main Liners took up arms against us and hired lawyers who forced a zoning hearing. Although the current zoning regulation made provision for congregational use, it soon became apparent that the contestants could literally tie us up in court for years, draining our financial resources. They had both money and the will to do whatever was necessary to prevent us from taking control of that property.

At the very first zoning board hearing, the courtroom was packed. News reporters and TV cameramen, and hundreds of people, who had been hearing rumors about us for quite awhile, became interested in the conflict, and came out to see for themselves what was happening. The famous Jewish author, Chaim Potok, was among them. We had many opportunities to interact with those present and give testimony to *Yeshua,* the first time we had talked openly about the Messiah.

Unfortunately, or so it seemed at the time, their strategy worked perfectly, and we were forced to drop out of the agreement of sale. We realized that it would probably take hundreds of thousands of dollars and years of court battles before we could win this case, and we simply did not have the resources to commit to such a legal fight - even if we had wanted to.

When we dropped the property, we rather expected the persecution to quiet down; instead, however, it intensified. The Jewish community was terrified at the thought of our somehow getting our own property and becoming a permanent fixture in the Philadelphia area. We were informed that our opponents had actually planted spies in our worship services to report any discussion we might have about available property for sale, and had detectives trail us whenever we went to look at a property. After the initial shock, we realized that, because of who we were, we would not gain possession of any building anywhere in the area without a legal fight.

In addition, the "anti-missionaries" had no end to their bag of dirty tricks. Not only were articles written against us, but ads were placed in newspapers and magazines designed to harass our people. The following ad, using our mailing address, appeared at least twice in the personal sex-ad section of *The Drummer*, a pornographic publication from Maryland:

3 RAVISHING WOMEN-Blonde, Brunette & Redhead. Blonde (Susan) for straight sex. Brunette (Linda) submissive to masterful men. Fiery Redhead (Debbie) for all S/M fantasies. All replies answered. A religious experience. Box 1024, Havertown, Pa. 19083

The women who were targeted in this ad were precious, born-again members of our congregation, and the mailing address given was that of Messianic Ministries, Inc., the organization that Marty and David had founded and of our campus ministry, as well. We saw later that *The Drummer's* advertisement-application form included the statement: "Publisher reserves the right to refuse to publish advertising which in its opinion does not conform to the reasonable standards of the DRUMMER/PLANET." We could only wonder what their "standards" might be.

Fourteen responses to the ad came in. Marty called some of them, telling the men who had responded that they were going to hell if they didn't repent of their evil desires. That must have made quite an impact!

In June 1979, Marty resigned permanently from the Executive Board of the MJAA, and Joel was elected presi-

Opposition

dent. I was thankful, for that was one burden Marty no longer needed to shoulder.

Negative coverage of our ministry continued relentlessly, in the newspaper, on radio and in TV-news coverage. On the front page of the November 1, 1979 issue of the *Main Line Jewish Exponent,* an article appeared under a large photograph of the deserted and neglected property we had tried to purchase. Headlined "The Storm on Latches Lane," it said in part:

> Beth Yeshua *is trying to obtain ... a large residential property ... as a "house of worship," missionary center and day school... . Though claiming to be authentic Jews who accept Jesus as the Messiah, we believe the group to be evangelical Christians who use the trappings of Judaism to entice young people - young Jews - into joining... . Community pressure generated against the application is our only weapon.*

Another article accused us of kidnapping a child and refusing to let him go until he accepted Jesus as his Savior!

The persecution eventually made us all "famous." One night, when two of our members attended the opera, during the intermission a man from New Jersey who was sitting beside them casually asked, "Where are you from?" When they replied, "Overbrook Park," the man said, "Oh yes, Overbrook Park! That's where those Messianic Jews live."

We comforted ourselves in knowing that battles like these and persecution such as we had experienced was not only what the early Messianic Jews had experienced in the Book of Acts, but what *Yeshua* Himself experienced during His days on earth. Little did we know that all of this "early" persecution was just a warm-up for the real thing!

CHAPTER NINETEEN

SUKKOT – THE GREAT FESTIVAL OF MESSIANIC JUDAISM

So the whole congregation of those who had returned from the captivity made booths. ... And there was very great gladness. Nehemiah 8:17, NKJ

1980-1984: PHILADELPHIA

How urgently we needed our own building! Between 1975 and 1980, there had been countless professions of faith at *Beth Yeshua* meetings and through personal ministry, including many non-Jews and scores of Jews. Because of our lack of facilities, however, many of those became lost in the shuffle.

Early in 1980, even without a building, we initiated two programs. David developed a concentrated, one-on-one, discipleship Bible study, especially for new Messianic Jews, using a series of twenty lessons emphasizing a personal walk with the Lord and answering questions especially important to young Jewish believers. The other program was a *Shamashim* (Deacon) program initiated by Marty, emphasizing leadership training, to encourage spiritual growth and maturity within the congregation. Many excellent leaders would eventually come out of that leadership program, including some future Messianic rabbis.

Still, we could not understand why we were not be-

Born a Jew...Die a Jew

ing shown any properties for sale near our homes. We had been meeting from hotel to hotel, and the place we were currently using was a rundown hotel with insufficient heating in the winter and insufficient air-conditioning in the summer. Plus there were many other "activities" going on upstairs that were incompatible with our purpose. We were there because we had run out of places that were large enough to hold us, and we were becoming desperate.

Then, one day, we heard some discouraging news through the grapevine. A waitress at a local restaurant reported to us a conversation she had inadvertently overheard. According to her, the main real-estate establishments in the area, which happened to be Jewish, were conspiring together with other elements of the Jewish community to keep us from acquiring any building anywhere near a Jewish neighborhood. The sympathetic waitress decided we should know that they had also entered into a conspiracy with other real-estate agents in the area, and that all had agreed privately that they would not show us any property within a 15-mile radius of the Jewish community. Apparently, they still had spies at our worship services, as well.

While some of our leaders continued the fruitless search for a building, in March 1980, Joe Finkelstein and I accompanied *Kol Simcha* to Toronto, Canada, where a Messianic synagogue called *Congregation Melech Yisrael* had scheduled them to present a Jewish song festival at the North Heights Secondary School in North York. The concert, though free, designated seating by ticket only. The congregation's spiritual leader, Hans Vanderwerff, warned his people ahead of time to expect strong opposition, but not to retaliate, reminding them that "*Yeshua* was defamed, but He reviled not, even when they called Him the son of the devil."

Sukkot – the Great Festival

His warning was both expedient and timely. More than two hundred protesters turned out in force, distributing leaflets entitled, "THE SOUL SNATCHERS ARE AT IT ... AGAIN!" The leaflets were "authenticated" by the York Jewish Student Federation, *B'nai Akiva,* the JDL, and the North American Jewish Students' Network. The JDL insignia, a star with a fist over it and the words "Never Again," was stamped at the bottom.

As Joe stood to introduce *Kol Simcha* to the audience, whistles and jeers came from the back of the room, and more than twenty Jewish protestors stood up and began their loud chanting: "Jews don't switch! Jews and Jesus don't mix!"

The police quickly escorted the protestors out, but it proved to be a ploy. Others, having gained entrance with forged tickets, had maintained their silence in order to disrupt and mock at intervals throughout the rest of the performance, loudly accusing our group of being Gentiles masquerading as Jews, as well as "spiritual Nazis" intent on annihilating the race. They whistled, they booed, they coughed, they mocked, they stamped their feet, they even staged fights across the seats and in the aisles.

Neither Joe nor any members of *Kol Simcha* reacted outwardly to the disturbance, but kept on emphasizing how much God loves the Jewish people - all of them!

One reporter from out of town, a professed unbeliever, said that one protester he interviewed, "was not coherent enough to reason with. He *hated* those Messianic Jews... . I [saw] religious oppression and hatred vented to an extent I never dreamed was possible in a free country. They were not there to protest, but to harass."

Kol Simcha's final song was the watchword of all Judaism: *Sh'ma Yisrael, Adonai Eloheynu. Adonai echad.* "Hear, O Israel, the Lord our God, the Lord is One."

They were given a standing ovation. Then, when one of the men blew the shofar before the final blessing, someone from the audience screamed, "Sacrilege! Sacrilege!"

During the concert, our smiling young people spent time conversing with the main audience inside, and also with the protestors outside. It was a wonderful night of witnessing, like reliving part of the Book of Acts. Many hearts were touched by love in the name of Messiah, even those of some of the most violent protestors.

We returned home with renewed zeal to find a property of our own, realizing that there was evidently only one way to counter the plot against us. We became faceless, anonymous real-estate prospects.

George Lane, a retired real-estate agent and member of our congregation, renewed his license and, with David, began to look for some properties anonymously.

George discovered an empty building for-sale-by-owner on Haverford Avenue, right around the corner from our house. It was a former restaurant, with a large parking lot but no grass, that had been sitting empty and neglected for months. Even though it was right in the heart of our community where the congregation had grown up, we had just never considered it. George had discovered that the owner, a Jewish person, wanted to sell quickly for cash.

One night after dark, two of our men, emulating Nehemiah as he covertly inspected the broken-down walls of Jerusalem, inspected the property by flashlight in order to evade the detectives always on our tails. We found the place to be absolutely a wreck and with little room for expansion, but it was suitable for us in layout and location, and we made an offer directly to the owner in the name of one of our congregants. Since we could not get a mortgage as a young congregation, the owner

Sukkot – the Great Festival

agreed to take one-third down and the balance within two years.

Before any of our detractors realized what was happening, in January 1981, money changed hands, and the contract was signed and sealed.

During this time, young Jeff Forman, raised as a Conservative Jew, received *Yeshua* as his Messiah, attended one of our meetings, and completely surrendered his life to the Lord. Jeff soon developed a deep and earnest prayer life, and began an intense study of the Word, not only under David and Marty, but also on his own. Marty discerned, in Jeff, a pastor's heart with a zeal for souls.

In April, after countless volunteer man-hours of scraping, scrubbing, fixing, rewiring, repainting, and rebuilding our own building, we moved in - accompanied by cameras, news reporters, and threats. The community was visibly and audibly upset.

As usual, there was a positive side to all this. Everybody already knew us, so we had many opportunities for interaction and chances to share the Good News of the Messiah.

Our first meeting inside our new building, a *Shabbat* service, was packed wall-to-wall with worshipers and the curious. It was a glorious time of celebration filled with joy and singing and dancing and praising God far into the night.

I soon began to see with my physical eyes the first fulfillment of the pink-cloud vision the Lord gave me after the *Kol Simcha* concert at the 1977 MJAA Conference, the vision about the creative force of Messianic Judaism flowing forth from Philadelphia. From then on, many young people with much creative talent, joined us. By then, *Lamb* was internationally known, having completed seven very popular albums and having appeared several times on television.

Kol Simcha was still going strong. And, by 1981, we had enough other gifted musicians to form our second singing group, the *Beth Yeshua Singers*, soon renamed *Shivat Zion* (Return to Zion), under the leadership of Rochelle Kronzek and, later, Steve Weiler. Then, in 1982, we formed our first messianic dance troupe, called *Tchiat Ami* (Salvation of My People), starting with four girls. The group debuted with a candle dance celebrating Hanukkah. They soon added four young men, with the vision of going out to introduce dance-worship into the Body.

But all was not well at home. One day, David and his friend John Pinto were panelling the walls in our basement, when Marty, who had been having trouble breathing recently, went down to see how they were doing. He had walked into the laundry room, when suddenly David and John heard him cry out. When they reached him, he was slumped against the laundry table, saying, "I don't know what's wrong; everything is blacking out." They called me, and I ran downstairs, took one look, then ran back upstairs and called to Dr. Robert Winer, who was there in the house, then frantically dialed 911. Meanwhile, David and John sat Marty down on a chair, then laid him flat on the floor, while his whole left side drew up and his face became paralyzed.

Dr. Winer ran past me down the stairs and tried to take Marty's pulse, but there was none. Marty had suffered a stroke, and Dr. Winer feared that he was already dead. Still upstairs, I called one person to start a prayer chain, then started calling others who came to mind who knew how to pray. Meanwhile, downstairs, it looked as if Marty had passed into eternity. There was no pulse, his entire left side of his body was paralyzed, his eyes were closed, and he was not moving and had not moved for several minutes.

Sukkot – the Great Festival

David was with him, when suddenly he opened his eyes and said, "I am healed by the resurrection power of *Yeshua!*" From that moment on, a healing process began that continued all night, until he was completely healed of what, later, we learned had been a major stroke, which should have taken his life.

The medics arrived and, by the time they got him to the hospital, he was only partially paralyzed on one side, with one eyelid drooping slightly. But he was sitting up, and within an hour, he was restored to 98 percent health! Once again God supernaturally healed our beloved Marty before our very eyes. Once again he should have died, but did not. Truly. God still had use for this remarkable man at this prophetic juncture in history!

Marty was in recuperation for three months and, during this time, David cut back on his campus activities to assume more rabbinic and pastoral responsibility within the congregation. The Board of Elders appointed him as Assistant Rabbi, and he preached at all the services for the next three months. When Marty was ready to resume his regular ministry schedule, he and David then shared the preaching and other pastoral responsibilities at *Beth Yeshua.*

Deep and concentrated congregational prayer over a period of months had stirred the people into glorious worship, and the services were packed. A powerful spirit of revival broke out. Marty was both amazed and thrilled to see what was happening, especially because of the number of souls being saved.

He shouldn't have been surprised. After all, he was the catalyst. He was the one who taught us the power of prayer for revival. He was the one who built the congregation with one hand, while being actively involved in building the international Messianic Movement with the other. He was the one in the center of every battle.

Meanwhile, as a family, we were expanding.

In March 1979, Joel had married Mindy Tatz, whom he met at a Messiah Conference. She was a Messianic Jew who had graduated in December from Stevens College in Columbia, Missouri. Mindy's parents flew us up to Chicago for a large wedding at the Ambassador-West Hotel. Then, the next day, we all returned to Philadelphia where they repeated their vows before the congregation, and we had an even larger reception at the Marriott Hotel.

David met a lovely, dark-haired, young Jewish believer named Debra Gershman at the June 1982 MJAA Conference at Messiah College in Grantham. The two fell in love and were married, October 9, 1983, at the Cherry Hill Hyatt Hotel in Cherry Hill, New Jersey. Very rapidly, Debbie became like me, a *rebbetzin* or rabbi's wife, teaching, praying, counseling and ministering with her husband within the congregation.

Hope also had met someone. He was tall, handsome Howard Edelstein, a young Messianic Jewish businessman, whom we all knew and loved. He and Hope were married, July 25, 1983, also at the Cherry Hill Hyatt Hotel in a beautiful, traditional Jewish wedding. For the finale, we all sang *Hallelujah,* a Messianic chorus. Every hand was raised in worship. Howard's mother "Barshie" commented later, "If I had known it was going to be like this, I would not have been afraid to invite all my friends!"

And so both our extended and immediate families grew upward and outward.

During 1979-1983, while Joel was president of the MJAA, the Messianic Movement split into two groups. We knew that God wanted the MJAA to continue in the vision that the Lord had shown us, not in a denomina-

Sukkot – the Great Festival

tional structure, not trying to "organize" God's revival, but rather as a loose alliance of multiplying, independent, self-supporting congregations, expanding worldwide, with no central denominational control, but under the exclusive authority of the Holy Spirit.

From 1980 on, Marty had been pressuring the younger members of the MJAA to start holding national conferences for Messianic leaders, rabbis, and heads of synagogues, to minister to the rabbis and congregations that were rapidly emerging in the Movement. Finally, in 1984, the first such conference was held in Philadelphia. Fourteen Messianic rabbis, representing fourteen different Messianic synagogues, attended, and Marty was the keynote speaker. Thus began, what would eventually become the "International Alliance of Messianic Congregations and Synagogues," with a membership today of over one hundred Messianic synagogues. Another of Marty's visions was coming to fruition.

Early one October morning, Marty, as usual, came down for a cup of his favorite English tea, then returned upstairs to pray. Alone at his old oak desk, in the privacy of his study, surrounded by his notes, his well-marked copy of Finney's book, and his many Bibles, he began a serious study of *Sukkot*, the last harvest festival on the Hebrew calendar. Marty felt impressed of the Lord that the time had come for us as Messianic Jews to keep *Sukkot*.

Historically known as the Jewish Feast of Tabernacles, *Sukkot* is our annual fall festival of thanksgiving for the harvest. During the seven days of *Sukkot*, Jewish people are supposed to live outdoors in branch-covered booths as a reminder of the flimsy huts in which their ancestors lived during their wanderings in the wilderness. *Sukkot* was prophetically the festival of the endtime harvest, the feast that the Gentiles would keep in the Millennium. The time of *Sukkot* was almost upon us.

Although we had never before celebrated *Sukkot* as a congregation, almost immediately we began building a big *"sukkah"* or "booth" in our parking lot from plywood and scrap lumber, a rough wooden frame covered by branches and leaves and draped with colorful paper chains. Many of the members of our congregation built booths in their back yards, or, if there was no back yard, their front yards.

We could not remember anyone from the Jewish community in Overbrook Park ever putting booths up before, but when we did, they did also.

During the festive week following, Marty and I were at home, while costumed members of *Kol Simcha* and other members of our congregation went from booth to booth singing and dancing to joyful Jewish songs. Many of our Messianic Jewish members came out of their homes and joined them, and the Holy Spirit spread joy throughout the neighborhood. There was singing and dancing in the streets and praising God at all the booths.

Crowds gathered. Even unbelieving Jews came out of their houses, wondering about the singing, and asking questions about Messiah. Someone called the police, who came, but who responded, "They're not hurting anything or anyone. We can't stop them." And they stayed to watch.

Someone phoned Marty at home to report that the Spirit of God had been poured out in Overbrook Park, and even some of the police officers were dancing! While Marty was listening to the message, he had a further thrilling revelation from God:

> *Sukkot, the last harvest festival, is to be the main festival of Messianic Judaism.*

Sukkot – the Great Festival

As thrilling as this was to us all, the fury against us had not abated, and we were still the targets of all sorts of harassment, persecution and dirty tactics. Frankly, we were getting used to the persecution and were learning how to handle it. We thought we had pretty much seen all of their dirty tricks, but *HaSatan* (the Devil) has been around a long time and has more "fiery darts" than we can imagine. We were soon to see things happen that we never imagined would happen.

Chapter Twenty

"If We Can Destroy *Beth Yeshua*..."

Open your mouth wide, and I will fill it.

Psalm 81:10

1984-1985: Philadelphia

In early June 1984, I went with twenty-seven others from our congregation on our own private tour of Israel. We returned home walking on air.

While we were gone, some very odd incidents were taking place around *Beth Yeshua*. We had always had opposition, but it now seemed to be taking a more sinister and personal turn. Vicious flyers were delivered to homes of believers; harassing calls were made in the middle of the night; parents of Messianic Jews were coming under persecution; rocks were thrown; threats were made. At first, these just seemed to be isolated incidents, but even before we left for Israel, they had begun to form into a new pattern of organized opposition with the specific goal of destroying us.

The following Sunday morning, June 10, I went out on our sun deck for my daily quiet time with the Lord. As I read the Scriptures for the day, certain words leapt from the pages and puzzled me:

When they bring you to synagogues and rulers and

authorities, do not worry how to defend yourself or what to say, for the Holy Spirit will teach you at the very moment what you ought to say.

Luke 12:11-12

As I arrived for the Sunday morning service (back then we had Friday and Sunday services, while today we have services on Friday night and Saturday morning), I could see a large group of people milling around outside our building and in the street. At first I wondered if there had been an accident. But as I drove closer, I saw that the strangers were all dressed in black, and were picketing our building. They carried huge signs accusing us of such crimes as kidnapping Jewish children. I was shocked. Lowering the car window, I overheard some of them threatening our members who were standing in the parking lot. The pickets were promising to either burn down our building, or continue harassing us until we agreed to turn it back into a restaurant.

These people were serious, and they had, once again, taken us by surprise. Since we had not anticipated such a situation, I wasn't sure exactly how to react. I simply drove slowly through their picket lines and went on into the building to join the worship service. An hour or so later, when we came back out, they were still there, still marching back and forth, still chanting, "Jews don't switch! Jews don't switch!" Some yelled at us and brandished their signs in our faces.

As we broke through their lines, one man on the street snarled at me, "I will lie, cheat, burn and even kill, if I have to, to keep one more Jew from walking into that building!"

I went home shaken. Later, I remembered that Marty had recently given a word of prophecy at one of our services in which he stated, "... this Messianic Movement

If We Can Destroy *Beth Yeshua*...

and Revival shall not be done in a corner ... ," in other words, God wanted His revival to be public knowledge.

When I reminded Marty of his prophecy, I also told him, and the young people who were in our house at the time, about the word the Lord had given me earlier that morning, that we were not to worry, that God was in it, that He would get glory from all of this. Together we prayed, commiting this situation into the hands of our Lord, *Yeshua.* He knew exactly how it felt to be harassed by enemies.

On another Sunday morning, a few weeks later, a bogus worshipper sat quietly through most of our meeting, before he stood up and shouted, "You are traitors to your people!" He wanted to speak further, but Marty quickly beckoned to our ushers and they escorted him out in a hurry.

From behind the pulpit, Marty explained his actions. "Other groups let people like him speak, but we believe that this is always counterproductive. Antagonists like him do not really want dialogue; they have no intention of discussing whether *Yeshua* was the Messiah or not. They come in only to disrupt, so we don't fool with them." We continued worshipping the Lord where we had left off in the service.

Twice more that summer, we were picketed. Meanwhile, God was showing us things in the Scriptures about how we were to act in the face of such persecution and how we could glorify Him through it:

> *Again I will build you, and you shall be built, O virgin Israel! Again you shall adorn yourself with timbrels and shall go forth in the dances of the merrymakers.* Jeremiah 31:4

The Lord was reminding us, through the Scriptures,

that when our people come back to the Land they dance. We had already heard news reports about Zionists who had come back to Israel. They were so happy to be home that they worked all day and danced the *hora* at night until they dropped. I felt that God was showing us, as Messianic Jews, Jews who were coming back to the Lord and back to our roots through the Messianic Movement, that we should do our ethnic dances, especially the *hora* and other Messianic dances to His glory, in the face of the demonstrators to show the joy and love of the Lord. Praise and worship releases the power of God, and some of the greatest victories in Scriptures occurred because men and women of God knew how to praise Him.

We knew from the Torah that our Jewish people had often joined together in worshipful victory dances of joy. Ezra and Nehemiah both danced in processions along the walls of Jerusalem, the city they were rebuilding. We would do it too, as long as we were able. We were also given the verse:

> *Surely the wrath of man shall praise Thee; further wrath wilt Thou restrain.* Psalm 76:10

We adopted these two special Scriptures about dancing versus the wrath of men as our watchwords, sure that the Lord would not allow our detractors to overpower us. As He made us strong, He would use our enemies' demonstrations to His glory and praise. We came to a strong faith that God had everything under His control.

The Lord showed us that we were never to answer in kind to those standing against us, never to shout back at them. That reaction would have been very easy in our frailty, but He wanted us to bless them, to return good for evil.

If We Can Destroy *Beth Yeshua*…

The third time we were picketed, we roped off our parking lot, then sent *Kol Simcha* out with each member dressed in a beautiful Israeli costume. With their tambourines and guitars, they danced and sang praises to God just a few feet from the pickets. After that, things seemed to quiet down for awhile, and we continued winning Jewish people to faith in their own Messiah.

As in the days of *Yeshua* on earth, apparently many of the Jewish leaders felt threatened, because later in the summer, posters and advertisements inveighing against us began appearing locally in Jewish newspapers, in the windows of some business establishments, on utility poles, and on construction walls announcing:

NATIONWIDE MARCH AGAINST BETH YESHUA

This new opposition was very serious. There were constant bomb threats and death threats; our tires were punctured, our children spit on, and items were stolen from around the synagogue. The antagonists would take down the license plate numbers of those attending our services, call their place of business and try to get them fired. We did not take all this lightly, but considered the threats serious enough that we were constantly in prayer against them.

For more than nine months, we seemed to be featured on local television or some other media at least once a week. We never got good press in the secular newspapers because the articles were written mostly by Jewish people. Television coverage was, for the most part, fair and sometimes even favorable. Well-known announcers occasionally showed up at our services where they had heard "something" was "going on" and had come to investigate. We called this our free Million-Dollar Advertising Campaign, because it gave us a chance to tell our story to literally hundreds of thousands of people, both Jewish and non-Jewish, throughout the entire Philadelphia area.

Then came the fourth and major protest against us. This was to be the big one, the "mother" of all anti-Messianic protests. This is the one that would topple *Beth Yeshua*, as thousands of anti-Messianics converged on Overbrook Park.

The protest was scheduled for Sunday, September 30, at eleven o'clock in the morning. We were warned, not unkindly, that people from all over the nation would congregate in Philadelphia to demonstrate against us on that day. Overnight, a full-blown billboard erected next to our property warned the community:

THERE IS A CULT IN YOUR NEIGHBORHOOD! GUARD YOUR CHILDREN!

Large posters put up all across the city, including one directly across the street from our front entrance, advertised the coming parade:

IMAGINE A WORLD WITHOUT JEWS! EXPOSE THE HOAX. WARN YOUR FELLOW JEWS AT A NATIONALLY COVERED MASS DEMONSTRATION AGAINST THE MESSIANIC MISSIONARY CULT, 'BETH YESHUA,' SUN. SEPT. 30, 11 AM.

One Jewish man, an unbeliever who owned a store in our neighborhood, said he was so ashamed of how the Jewish leaders were harassing us, that he wanted to help. He wanted to give us something, but all he had was a

If We Can Destroy *Beth Yeshua*…

big roll of poster paper. Could we use it? Our young people quickly unrolled the poster paper across the floor and began painting. When they finished, they posted the fruits of their labor, several two-by-forty-foot signs, across the top of our building. They proclaimed:

WE ARE PROUD TO BE JEWISH, AND WE ARE NOT ASHAMED OF THE MESSIAH!

THE CONSTITUTION GUARANTEES US FREEDOM OF WORSHIP!

MESSIANIC JEWISH CONGREGATIONS PRESERVE JEWISH LIFE!

I WAS BORN A JEW; I WILL DIE A JEW!

LEADERS CAN BE WRONG; THINK FOR YOURSELF!

YOU ARE BEING ANTI-SEMITIC-WHY?

The protestors' parade permit allotted them four hours, from eleven in the morning until three in the afternoon. What they could not know was that, twenty-four hours earlier, God had given both Marty and me another word to reinforce His earlier promise:

In the transgression of an evil man there is a snare, but the righteous man sings and rejoices.
Proverbs 29:6

We remembered that during a previous demonstration we had prayed, and it had rained. We considered that to be such a merciful show of God's power, that again we prayed for rain, and we prayed, and we prayed. But the next day broke bright and clear, a gorgeous, sunny fall day, registering a comfortable 70° Fahrenheit. (Amusingly, we later learned that a hurricane had been coming up the coast, but Pat Robertson of CBN in Virginia Beach, Virginia, had prayed it out to sea!) It never reached us in Philadelphia, and the weather could not have been better.

Our own people showed up early that morning, and so did the members of several local churches who came to stand with us. By mid-morning, we had about five hundred people, including visitors, inside our building, many holding hands and praying against the demonstration, while David attempted to conduct a service. Because of Marty's health, we had decided that he should stay home and pray, and we would periodically call and apprise him of the situation.

Most of the marchers were gathering at the local Jewish Community Center two blocks away. Jewish people had been bussed in from all over Philadelphia, and from as far away as New York, Baltimore, Washington, and other places along the East Coast. The marchers numbered about a thousand.

It was intimidating and somewhat scary. The atmosphere was electrically charged and dangerous.

It had come to our attention, from sources within the Jewish community, that this group of "anti-Messianics" that was leading this march had decided to make *Beth Yeshua* their trial balloon. If they could destroy *Beth Yeshua* through intimidation, threats, and demonstrations, then they would move on to other Messianic synagogues

If We Can Destroy *Beth Yeshua*...

throughout the United States and do the same. This was their "game plan" for destroying the Messianic Movement.

Earlier, we had cordoned off our property behind a chain barrier running along the edge of the sidewalk, separating the curious crowd and out-of-towners from us. That way, none of them could push over onto our property, and none of us could easily cross over to them. The chain also nicely defined a stage area for our counter-demonstration.

Before eleven o'clock, while we were already talking with some of the gathering crowd, several shiny, black Cadillacs and two 20-foot-long flat-bed trucks rolled up and parked directly across the street from our property. As the minute hand approached the hour, the police cordoned off the entire block at both ends, and turned to watch.

While they watched us, we watched the Orthodox rabbis. With their black coats and hats, *pa'ot* (side curls) and beards, they surveyed the crowd of hundreds of onlookers thronging our street. Their assistants hooked the loudspeakers up to their portable electric generators, then tested for sound.

We talked quietly among ourselves, and waited.

The march began.

The protestors marched down our street from the Jewish Community Center, stopping traffic along the way. They had signs such as "No Nazis in Skokie (Illinois) and no Messianic Jews in Overbrook Park." It was a massive gathering.

The police were out in full force, along with some friendly security guards we had hired to keep the peace. All three major television stations were there along with a slew of other reporters from along the East Coast, all waiting to see what would happen.

Born a Jew...Die a Jew

As the thousand or so marchers descended on *Beth Yeshua* for a full day of persecution, we had planned a counter-demonstration. We put our speakers outside, cranked them up and planned on broadcasting the praise and worship service that was going on inside. We hoped that this might disrupt their demonstration, as our sound system was so much more powerful than theirs! Admittedly, it was not much of a plan, but it seemed to be all that we could think of at the time.

At eleven sharp, the first rabbi stepped up to the microphone to begin his harangue against us. At that moment, an idea came to me. I went inside and suggested to David that, instead of just blasting our praise and worship service out over the loudspeakers, why not have some singers and dancers come outside and let the worship be visible to everyone. The television cameras were sure to pick it all up, as it would seem so incongruous - in light of the hostilities being demonstrated against us.

David concurred, and we got ready to send about twenty or so dancers outside, like Jehoshaphat sending the singing Levites out into battle before the army of the Lord (1 Chronicle 20). While the rabbis and "anti-Messianics" tried to give their speeches, lively Messianic Jewish music blared through our speakers and beautifully costumed performers ran from our building, singing and dancing as they went. They were young, handsome men, dresed in royal-blue, cotton trousers, loose, long-sleeved, braid-trimmed, immaculate, white-cotton shirts with colorful fringed sashes, with *yarmulkes* on their heads; and beautiful, young girls with flowers in their hair, wearing colorful, flowing dresses with brightly patterned scarves, and white slippers. The crowd was dumbfounded.

Whatever the people had come to witness, it was not

If We Can Destroy *Beth Yeshua*…

happening. Instead, they were suddenly audience to a very attractive, performing group of over twenty exuberant young people, full of excitement, radiant with love, and in total unity. They performed gloriously. With their fresh, beautiful faces aglow, some even came to a microphone that we had set up and began to witness to the crowd about *Yeshua*'s being not only the Jewish Messiah, but their own personal Savior as well.

Within a very short time, the atmosphere was changed by the Power of God!

David came out to see what was going on and was amazed at the anointing of praise and worship that was sweeping throughout the area! He went back inside and asked for another hundred or so volunteers, telling them, "Just go out and praise theLord!"

Eventually, the entire congregation poured out from the building to join in the singing and dancing and praising God, with no show of animosity, only love for the curious crowd.

The more we praised God, the more the *Ruach HaKodesh* fell on all of us, the protestors included. The anger in the crowd rapidly melted away and was replaced by an extreme spiritual hunger to know more about this fascinating group. The Jewish leaders of the march were so shocked by the sudden turn of events that they wrapped up their planned four-hour program after only forty-five minutes and told all their people to go back to the Jewish center and not to talk to any of the Messianic Jews.

That was a mistake. Those people had come too far to be told not to talk to anyone, and Jewish people, in general, are too independent for that! Besides, there was a joyous and festive air over the city that day, and nobody wanted to leave because of it.

Born a Jew...Die a Jew

Drawing our own happy children into the circles, we danced and sang, praying in our hearts that these dear Jewish people, who had come to watch and perhaps to mock, would stay and be blessed, would experience our joy, and desire what we had in the Lord. One of our songs that struck a chord in their hearts, especially the hearts of the shocked Orthodox rabbis still watching, was *Blow the Shofar in Zion*.

At times our dancers would stop to rest, and. our young men would preach to the crowd about *Yeshua*, or witness one-on-one. No one in the crowd showed any disrespect, and hundreds stayed to sing and dance and clap their hands, and listen to the messages about the Messiah.

One charming woman, who had been bussed in from out of state, put out her hand and said, "Help me! I want to get over on your side of this chain and dance with you. I came down here, all the way from New York, to participate in this demonstration, and now I want to demonstrate - but with you."

One of our young men took her hand in his and held the chain down with his foot as she stepped over. As far as we know, she never did understand what the parade was supposed to accomplish. We do know that she ended up having a good time, celebrating with us.

The faces of some of the visiting rabbis reflected their shock and amazement, while quite a few bewildered and honest spectators came over to us and asked why we believed that *Yeshua* was the Messiah. We were able to point out, in their own Bibles, some important texts, such as Isaiah 7:14 and 53:1-12.

When the frustrated promoters finally left, only about a hundred people left with them. Everyone else stayed. How those men must have regretted ever planning that protest in the first place!

If We Can Destroy *Beth Yeshua*…

Even some Orthodox rabbis stayed to talk with us and did not leave until after 7 PM. Some of them confessed that they had never before taken note of the Messianic prophecies in Isaiah 53 or Daniel 9.

It was two in the morning before the last of the crowd finally disbursed. As we were getting ready to leave, we noticed a rabbi from New York still sitting in his Cadillac across the street. He was obviously very distraught. As it turned out, he had blown his horn so long in protest, trying to drown out the worship, that he had run his battery down. One of our men graciously and politely jump-started his car for him, and red-faced, he drove away.

All-in-all, what started off as perhaps the worst day of our ministry had turned into one of the most wonderful days we ever had. We felt as though we were reliving the Book of Acts. David called it "our largest service to date" - well over 1,500 people, including the demonstrators. The whole affair was written up in the press, and given time on three television news programs. One report included a film clip of a man stepping over the chain to join us. We believe the Lord did a mighty work in the hearts of many that day, in people we may never meet again until we rejoice together in Heaven.

As much as anything else that ever happened in our ministry, this event defined us and brought about permanent changes that would affect our ministry for years to come.

The backbone of the nearly yearlong demonstrations and persecutions ended almost immediately. Now, years later, we hardly hear a peep out of the Jewish opposition. They now realize that they gave us publicity for nearly a year that normally would have cost us millions in advertising dollars if we had been forced to buy it.

This makes them almost afraid to even mention us. They certainly don't want to give us any more free advertising!

Another major effect of the demonstration is that it brought us out of the closet, so to speak. Up until this point, from 1975 to 1980, we had maintained a kind of "bunker mentality," defensive and cautious about everything we did and said because of all the persecution. In some respects, the persecutors had succeeded in silencing us. After that day in 1984, however, we have come out boldly and done things we never had the courage to do before. We now go boldly wherever we want, and are not afraid of media coverage and even opposition. We are constantly looking to turn our city "upside-down" for the Lord!

Because of the experience of that day, we now know that we could handle an immense amount of persecution and grow from it! The "anti-Messianics" are sorry to have seen this dramatic change in *Beth Yeshua*.

Finally, we feel that the Lord stopped, at our doorstep, an attack of the Adversary aimed at the entire Messianic movement. If those demonstrators had been able to destroy us, I have no doubt they would have tried this same pattern elsewhere. Because we were larger and stronger than most other Messianic congregations, God wanted us to handle this battle for the sake of the whole movement. It was our pleasure to do so.

A week after the incident, it was again time for *Sukkot*. Still feeling high from God's victory over the protest parade, we decided to continue making our statement to the community. Once again, we erected a booth of branches in our parking lot and held a big outdoor *Sukkot* celebration with our costumed singers and dancers and lots of free food. We set out chairs for the Jewish neigh-

If We Can Destroy *Beth Yeshua*...

bors passing by, some of whom stopped to *nosh* with us, and listen to our testimonies to the incomparable goodness of God. They were some of the very people who had demonstrated against us such a short time before.

Beth Yeshua, Messianic Judaism and the Messiah *Yeshua* were out of the closet for good! Truly, when God does a work, the devil does not have a chance!

As the Psalmist proclaimed:

> *Weeping may endure for a night, but joy cometh in the morning.* Psalm 30:5, KJV

Chapter Twenty-One

Rabbi Martin, Rabbi David

In Him every believer is absolved from everything from which you could not be absolved by the Law of Moses.
Acts 13:39

1985: Philadelphia

By 1985, David had already assumed much of the oversight of the congregation, and my heart swelled with deep gratitude to God for continuing to use each member of the Chernoff family in this last-day movement. Joel, teamed up with Rick Coghill, was introducing Messianic music worldwide through Lamb. Hope was indispensable to the ministry as secretary in the congregational office, as well as being involved with youth work.

Marty, a fiery evangelist, always preached like one. Whenever he prepared his sermons, he first wrote down the message he thought the Lord wanted him to give, then sat quietly in his study waiting for the Lord to speak to him. Whatever supernatural knowledge or wisdom or counsel the Lord impressed upon his heart to present to his people, never specifically aimed at any one person, he inserted into his notes. Often, many in the congregation would come forward afterwards and say, "I felt as if you were preaching right at me."

Marty's fiery manner sometimes made me flinch. Basically his preaching was very sharp and to the point, straight from the Word of God, without compromise, but then he would say something humorous, and the sweetened word would strike home. He could preach fire and brimstone, then throw out a pun, and everyone would laugh. He often poked fun at something he did not like, something very sad or deeply serious or painfully disappointing, turning it into a joke, a thing to laugh at - a very Jewish trait and a very effective one. Masterful at hiding negative emotions, reticent to display affection in public, he always loved a good joke.

One quiet afternoon in September, I listened to one of Marty's latest preaching tapes, bracing myself and thinking, *I wonder how far he's going to go with this strong message before he makes a pun.* But he never did. This message was different, unyielding, totally without humor, not typical of my fun-loving husband, not his style. *Why does he sound so intense?* I wondered and I mused, *It's not as though he hasn't seen at least partial fulfillment of his major vision. He has seen it.*

My mind wandered off through the incredible events of the last few years, and I thought, *Surely, the Jesus Movement and the parallel Messianic Jewish Movement together comprise the greatest, most recent revival in the history of America!* Perhaps while it was unfolding, we, as a family, were too close to the very vortex to recognize the phenomenon clearly for what it was, and how deep and how wide its influence was on the American scene.

Marty, to my way of thinking, had no reason to sound so intense on the tape. He had witnessed marvelous things, multitudes of Jewish people pouring into the Kingdom, running to the God of their fathers, stretching out their arms to embrace and bring in their own people, then reaching back to reclaim their Jewish roots.

But, as humble and gentle as Marty was by nature, when God showed him something, he could preach it

Rabbi Martin, Rabbi David

with fire, turning neither to the right nor to the left. For example, when others in the Movement first discerned in their spirits that God was creating something new, moving us, as a group, in an entirely new and different direction, many floundered trying to analyze it in their heads, debating among themselves.

For instance, some said, "Messianic Judaism is the fourth branch of Judaism: Orthodox, Reform, Conservative, and now Messianic."

"No!" Marty declared. "You are wrong! This is not one of four branches of Judaism! Messianic Judaism, by itself, is God's true biblical Judaism! There is no other!" And he never swerved from that conviction.

By early summer, our synagogue numbered about three hundred members, while regularly attracting countless others to the Lord. Our children, happily married to God's choice for them, were all three deeply involved in the congregation and the ministry, helping to shape and to mold the future of Messianic Judaism. Each time one of them moved out of our home, my husband complained to me, "This house is too empty," and we would invite a few young men of leadership quality to come for a season to share our home and ministry.

In June, as was our custom, we were getting ready to go to the Annual MJAA Conference at Messiah College, planning to leave a couple days early to get out there and rest, but Marty wasn't feeling well in the morning, so he asked Dr. Robert Winer, who was staying with us at the time, to check his heart.

Bob agreed, and his heart sank when he sensed the results. He did not tell Marty what he suspected, but merely said, "Marty, I think before you go to the conference, you need to check with your heart doctor."

While Mark Dayan drove Marty to the hospital for a quick, cursory checkup, I went to the drugstore for a few last minute things needed for our trip. I left our suitcases lying open but ready for us to pick up and leave as soon as we both returned home.

After I came back, Marty called me from the hospital. "I think you had better come. The doctor wants me to stay in the hospital for more tests."

David and I rushed to the hospital, where they had already assigned Marty a room. His somber doctor took us aside. He said, "Marty has cardiomyopathy, a complication from his earlier heart attacks. He has been literally living and working on only half a heart for the past twelve years, and it has suddenly started enlargeing. He has only about six or eight more months to live. I want to put him in Intensive Care right away."

Despite his physical condition, Marty decided to attend the Messiah '85 Conference. His anointing never faltered. Even after we came back home to our congregation for special post-conference meetings, the power of God flowed mightily through Marty's hands, and people were healed, filled with the Spirit, and filled with joy, as he ministered to them. Those meetings often lasted until one o'clock in the morning.

All summer, he continued to minister in the congregation, but towards September he began feeling weaker day by day. In October, when he was again hospitalized, once his heart stopped completely. He had no memory of it, and was never told that he had actually died for a short time. But I knew, and I asked him, "Marty, have you had any visions or dreams or revelations since you've been in here?"

"Yes, I did!" he said, seemingly surprised that I would ask him. "Myriads of angels in Heaven."

"Did you by any chance see the Lord?"

"Yes, and I knew it was the Lord! He was standing there surrounded by those angels."

Rabbi Martin, Rabbi David

During the two weeks he was hospitalized, Marty came in and out of consciousness. When he was conscious, and even sometimes when he was not, he continued giving wise, spiritual counsel for me to deliver to some of the members of our congregation, such as:

"Tell that couple contemplating marriage that God will bless them only if they put Him first."

"Remind the Elders that there are still four hundred thousand Jewish people right here in Philadelphia who need to be saved. Tell them to focus on revival."

What kept going through my mind was, *He gets sick and God heals him. He gets sick and God heals him. He's like a boxer, a strong man getting knocked down by his opponent, but always getting back up. He's had miraculous healings - never a recurrence of cancer since his bout with it in 1973. God is always glorified when He heals Marty.*

This time, however, Marty never left the hospital. He had finished his course. His heart gave out, and he was transported into the glorious presence of his Messiah, Whom he had served steadfastly for forty-five of his sixty-seven years. We were shocked, never having believed for one moment that he would die at the age of 65. We always envisioned Marty like Moses who lived to 120 years of age with *"his eyes not dimmed nor his strength abated."* But it was not to be. Marty's exhausted heart finally gave out on Sunday morning, October 27, 1985, and his mantle fell upon the 34-year-old shoulders of our son David.

Even in death Marty continued to cause controversy within the Jewish community. We had already buried a number of people through the local Jewish funeral homes and using the local Jewish cemetery. After Marty died, we agreed on which home to use and contacted them. They, in turn, agreed to find us a cemetery with an available and suitable plot. When they took the body to the

Born a Jew...Die a Jew

funeral home, we followed and proceeded to make the arrangements. But news travels fast.

When a certain rabbi who lived near us found out that the controversial Messianic Jewish Leader and Rabbi, Martin Chernoff, had died, he quickly warned all the Jewish cemetery owners, "... on the grounds that Chernoff, though born a Jew, had forfeited his right to a Jewish burial when he became a Baptist minister and espoused the belief that Jesus is the Messiah."

After that proclamation, if any one of them accepted Marty's body for burial, he was *meshumid,* and the rabbis would declare that cemetery "nonkosher." Consequently, at midnight, the cemetery owner phoned to tell us that he was sorry, but they could not bury Marty the next day.

Meanwhile, Messianic Jewish leaders and friends were already arriving from around the country and from around the world to attend the funeral. Frantically, we got lawyers on the case, but to no avail; no Jewish cemetery would accept his body for burial. In the wee hours, we finally contacted a nonsectarian cemetery owner, who agreed to have a grave ready the next morning.

As a result, a one hundred-car caravan of Messianic Jews and other believers followed the hearse carrying Marty's body through the streets of Philadelphia to a grave in nonsectarian ground. Thus, mourners from all over the world were present to pay their last respects to Martin Chernoff, pioneer, visionary and leader, who had departed this life and gone to meet his Messiah and Lord in the same way he had lived, amid turmoil and controversy.

Five days later, on October 30, the outrageous controversy resumed on the front page of Section B, in *The Philadelphia Inquirer,* headlined: "Messianic Leader in City is Denied Jewish Burial." The article said in part:

Rabbi Martin, Rabbi David

David Gotlib, who runs the Jewish Resource Center in Overbrook Park, said that he did not understand why members of Beth Yeshua would have assumed it was possible to have Mr. Chernoff buried in a Jewish cemetery.

The article went on to say that the Jewish Resource Center, funded by the Federation of Jewish Agencies of Greater Philadelphia, had been *"established in February to counteract the influence of Beth Yeshua in the neighborhood."*

On the same day, *The Philadelphia Daily News* ran an article on page 4, headlined, "Even Death Can't Bury Controversy." The next day, *The Main Line Times* ran their article on page 13, headlined, "Messianic Rabbi Denied Burial."

The subject did not end there. On November 8, *The Jewish Exponent* ran their article on page 5, headlined, "Messianic Denied Jewish Burial," in which the president of *Har Jehuda* was quoted as saying that "the only logical decision was to refuse him burial because we also knew that Chernoff's grave would become a shrine to his congregants - and we didn't want that here."

As a family, we felt that this huge controversy was a fitting end to Martin M. Chernoff's life. Even in death he was stirring up controversy in the Jewish community, forcing them to address the issue of Jews who believe in *Yeshua* and even *Yeshua* Himself.

He died the way he had lived, and he would have been pleased!

Many Scriptures came to our mind when Marty passed away. One of them was from Isaiah:

The righteous man perishes ... no one lays it to heart that the righteous man is taken away before calamity comes; he enters peace. They rest each in his bed who has gone on his upright way.   Isaiah 57:1-2

From this passage we felt that Marty had finished the battles the Lord had ordained for him. He had fought the good fight and was a weary warrior going home for a good, long rest!

Another passage which spoke to Marty's death was from John's Revelation:

Blessed are the dead which die in the Lord from now on. Yes, says the Spirit, that they may rest from their labors; for the results of their labors follow them.
          Revelation 14:13

Truly Marty's *labors* have continued - through his children, his spiritual children, his teaching and vision that have become foundational to much of the Messianic Movement today.

The passage that I decided to put on Marty's gravestone was the one that said it all for me. The only truly important thing in Marty's life was that he, like King David before him, *"serv[ed] the purpose of God in his own generation"* (Acts 13:36).

Good night, my husband, my love, my best friend.

Chapter Twenty-Two

New Wine to Come

Ask from the LORD rain in the time of the latter rain. ... He will give you rain in abundance with vegetation in every field.   Zechariah 10:1

Post 1985: Philadelphia

The fruit of Marty's ministry continues to bring forth life for many. Just as the physical regathering to the Land of Israel had its *halutzim* (pioneers), so Israel's spiritual restoration, Messianic Judaism and its revival, had its pioneers, as well. That is how I remember my husband, Martin M. Chernoff - as a pioneer in this movement for the glory of God.

Marty saw God developing among our Jewish people a spontaneous, powerful, all-encompassing revival, something no human agency could have implemented. God Himself was the Prime Mover, taking all of us in directions that we could not have planned by ourselves. The pattern was God's pattern alone:

1. The Holy Spirit endued the revival with a supernatural life of its own.
2. Leadership sprang up from among the youth themselves, especially those who first accepted *Yeshua* as their Messiah in the 70s and 80s. As Jeremiah prophesied: *"Their prince shall be from*

among themselves, and their ruler shall come forth from their midst" (Jeremiah 30:21).

3. They hungered to go back to biblical Jewish roots, a oneness with their own people and a desire to share the Messiah with them. As Zephaniah predicted: *"I will gather those belonging to you who sorrow for the sacred assembly [Jewish festivals], who have borne the burden of reproach [for being Jewish]"* (Zephaniah 3:18).
4. They established their own worship centers with strictly Jewish forms of worship - Messianic praise with new music, much from the *Tanach*, especially the Psalms, and dancing with tambourines and guitars, incorporating simplicity, spontaneity and the love of Hebrew.
5. They replaced church-related holidays with biblical festivals and holy days: Passover, *Shavuot, Rosh Hashanah, Yom Kippur, Sukkot, Hanukkah, Purim* and even moved back to worshipping on the Sabbath, the seventh day of the week.

While incorporating these innovations, Marty often stood alone against attempts to lead the movement into becoming a formal, man-made denomination; against attempts to promote others into prideful positions of supreme authority; and against forming a tight-structured Messianic worship liturgy drawn from dead traditions, thereby giving it a stifling foothold not born of the Spirit. He believed in letting the Holy Spirit take full control, that when a movement becomes controlled or organized, it ceases to be a revival.

Marty's concern was for revival, letting the Holy Spirit keep control, seeking guidance on our knees, beseeching God for the latter rain.

New Wine to Come

For the land which you are entering to possess is not like the land of Egypt ... where you could ... water it with your foot ... . No, the land you are reaching to possess ... depends for water upon the rains from heaven, a land over which the LORD your God watches ... . Deuteronomy 11:10-12

The temptation today is the easy way of going back to Egypt for help, borrowing from the world and its ways, putting confidence in working the foot, rather than bowing the knee. Any Holy Spirit revival spontaneously and sovereignly cuts across this human tendency. There is no mightier corrective to human methods than a heaven-sent outpouring. Who would want to continue working the foot pump, when Heaven is pouring down a great shower of blessings?

Marty saw three steps of preparation necessary for revival:

1. Breaking up the fallow, previously fruitful, but now hard and unproductive, ground; rain on hard, unbroken ground will erode the soil and wash away any seeds.
2. Watching, fasting, and praying fervently until the rains from Heaven come.
3. Believing God for the promised harvest.

Of these three steps, breaking up the fallow ground was our most difficult task: waiting before Him, letting Him put His finger on our sins, hindrances, our apathy and worldliness which grieve the Holy Spirit. We had to repent, ask forgiveness, and, only then, go on.

Breaking up the fallow ground in our hearts and lives is our responsibility *"until He comes and rains righteous-*

ness upon you" (Hosea 10:12). The prophet Jeremiah admonished: *"Do not sow among thorns"* (Jeremiah 4:3).

Over the Land of Israel there are two major rains, both necessary, and both fraught with deep spiritual implications. During the early rain of October-November, the ground is softened. This is when the farmers plow, prepare the soil, and plant the seed - in anticipation of the harvest. This "early rain" continues off and on until the spring dry period. Then come the "latter rains," a steady downpour vital to an abundant harvest at the appointed season for reaping. Spiritually, both rains are conditioned by our obedience: Without preparedness, we could miss the entire revival-harvest, something we are determined not to do.

Meanwhile, our family continues to grow and expand, with many, precious, grandchildren who are being raised in our Messianic academy and serving the Lord. We all rejoice together during family meals at the big house on Sherwood Road. Each Tuesday night we have dinner in the dining room at two big separate tables, one for seating the adults, house guests and drop-ins, and the other for the many grandchildren of Marty and Yohanna Chernoff! Marty would have loved every minute of it, and I am sure that he is pleased that we continue this tradition.

I am both humbled and joyful that all of my children are believers and are Messianic leaders in this end-time Jewish revival, Messianic Judaism.

The ministry continues to grow and expand, as well, reaching out to touch the Messianic Movement worldwide.

Joel wonks full-time as the General Secretary of the Messianic Jewish Alliance of America (MJAA), as it spreads its influence over the world, touching and en-

New Wine to Come

couraging Messianic Jews everywhere, reaching into Israel with many opportunities to witness for Messiah. He also remains strongly involved in Messianic music - composing, singing and ministering in concerts on a regular basis.

David is now Senior Messianic Rabbi of Congregation *Beth Yeshua* and envisions a day soon when we will all experience a new outpouring of the Spirit and mega-Messianic synagogues. He has been involved in the rabbinic arm of the MJAA, the International Alliance of Messianic Congregations and Synagogues (IAMCS). He writes, speaks on the movement and hosts a weekly television show about Messianic Judaism.

Our daughter, Hope Chernoff Edelstein, remains strongly involved in the local congregation as well as serving the Lord as the Executive Director of the Young Messianic Jewish Alliance of America, working with youth, singles and young couples. Hope sees another youth revival like the one in the 70s coming in the near future.

In addition to my three children being in the ministry, my daughter-in-law, Debbie Chernoff, David's wife, has become a full-time spiritual *rebettzin* alongside her husband, teaching, counselling and ministering. She has also become a national teacher of the women in the movement.

As I rejoice in the Lord for my family, my mind cannot help thinking back and being amazed at how large my spiritual family is. To see so many spiritual leaders in the movement who came out of our ministry in Cincinnati and in Philadelphia is one of the greatest joys Marty and I could ever have.

At the time of this writing, I am still very active, serving Messiah locally and speaking nationally, tearing down strongholds in the Spirit for the rebirth of Israel -

the new wave of revival. It is exciting to see what God is doing in the End of Days.

Aside from my immediate family, I rejoice for the larger family in the Lord and stand amazed at just how large that spiritual family (we call it *Mishpoche,* in Yiddish) has become. Seeing so many spiritual leaders in the movement who came out of our ministry, at *Beth Messiah* in Cincinnati and at *Beth Yeshua* in Philadelphia, is one of the greatest joys Marty and I could ever have. I feel a special warmth and closeness to them, although we were not able to train them all and send them all out. Some we trained and sent, and others went out on their own and were used of God. I would like to recognize them now.

From our days in Cincinnati:

1. Rabbi Jeff Adler (*Simchat Yeshua,* Indianapolis, Indiana; national leader in the Union of Messianic Jewish Congregations, UMJC)
2. Phyliss Adler Blackburn (she and her husband Tom are the spiritual leaders of a Messianic synagogue in Upland, California)
3. Bruce Adler (Elder, *Beth Messiah*, Cincinnati, Ohio; former YMJA President)
4. Rabbi Robert Cohen (he and his wife, Roxanne, who is from our congregation in Philadelphia, minister at *Beth Jacob* inJacksonville, Florida; Robert is currently MJAA President)
5. Mark Dayan (nationally known worship leader; member of the *Kol Simcha* Messianic singing group)
6. Elliot and Joyce Klayman (lawyer and Elder in Columbus, Ohio; leader in the UMJC)
7. Fran Rosenfarb Feldman (she and her husband

New Wine to Come

Larry have ministered in Messianic congregations since the early 1970s)
8. Rabbi Joseph Rosenfarb (Virginia, Ba.; chemist, leader in the UMJC)
9. Dr. Robert Winer (neurologist; leader, with his wife Tara in *Beth Yeshua*; Robert is a writer, international speaker and member of the MJAA Executive Committee)

From *Beth Yeshua* in Philadelphia:

1. Rabbi Joseph and Debbie Finkelstein (Messianic pioneers before we came to Philadelphia; Assistant Rabbi at *Beth Yeshua*; member of MJAA Executive Committee leader of internationally-known singing group *Kol Simcha*)
2. Jeff and Diane Lowenthal (Elder, at *Beth Yeshua* in Philadelphia; lawyer; member MJAA Executive Committee)
3. Rabbi Michael and Rachel Wolf *(Beth Messiah*, Cincinnati, Ohio; past President MJAA; currently member of MJAA Executive Committee; writes and produces Messianic videos)
4. Rabbi Jeff and Janet Forman (City of David, Toronto, Canada; formally Assistant Rabbi of *Beth Yeshua* for ten years)
5. Steve and Pat Weiler (leadership at Beth *Yeshua*; leader of the nationally known singing group *Shivat Tzion*; principal of *Halutzim* Academy and leader in the Messianic educational field)
6. Rabbi Bruce and Debbie Cohen (Manhattan, New York; Messianic author and composer; worked for MJAA for many years)
7. Rabbi David and Helene Rosenberg (Long Island, New York; Northeast Regional Director of the

International Alliance of Messianic Congregations and Synagogues)
8. Rabbi Jan and Marlene Rosenberg (central New Jersey; past members of *Kol Simcha*, ministering internationally for years)
9. Hank Rich (leader at *Beth Yeshua*; businessman; member of the MJAA Executive Committee
10. James Morse (member of *Beth Yeshua*; past YMJA President; traveling speaker and evangelistic minister)
11. John Rose (leader *Beth Yeshua*; local and national songleader and singer)

Even as I look back on what has transpired and rejoice, I look forward with even greater excitement for the future; for since Marty passed away, the foundation he laid has been built upon, has grown, and has spread out throughout the world.

Congregation Beth Yeshua has grown, is branching out into many new ministries and is looking forward to thousands coming into the kingdom in the near future. The MJAA has blossomed internationally in its ministry and impact. The IAMCS has established itself as a strong rabbinic organization, ministering to both congregations and rabbis worldwide.

The End-time Jewish revival has not peaked by any stretch of the imagination. We have not yet seen the full outpouring of the *Ruach HaKodesh* upon the Jewish people, or the nations, for that matter in final latter rain revival as promised in the book of Joel. Those in the Messianic Movement must keep their eyes on the goal and not be distracted to the right or to the left. Many who have been saved in this spiritual awakening are being lured away by self, sin, pride and the cares of this

New Wine to Come

life. Let us fervently pray that the work God has begun among His Chosen People will continue and intensify.

> *Ask from the Lord rain in the time of the latter rain.*
> Zechariah 10:1

> *I will make them and the places around My hill a blessing, sending rains to come down in their season; there shall be showers of blessing.*
> Ezekiel 34:26

We must not be filled with the old wine only, but thirsty for the new wine, for a mighty move of the Spirit in fresh, new ways. When He comes, let us be spiritually prepared to recognize Him, and all be willing to be *chalutzim*, ready to move with Him.

> *If I shut up heaven so there is no rain ... among My people, and My people, who are called by My name, humble themselves and pray and seek My face and turn from their evil ways, then I will hear from heaven and forgive their sin and heal their land. My eyes shall be open and My ears attentive to prayer from this place.*
> 2 Chronicles 7:13-15

AND THE END IS NOT YET!

Chapter Twenty-Three

A Prophecy
By Rabbi Martin Chernoff

In many ways, this is Marty's book, and it should be ended with his words. The following important prophetic utterance was delivered by him during the service on Friday night, April 4, 1984, in *Beth Yeshua* Synagogue in Philadelphia, Pennsylvania, one week before the first of the four overt demonstrations against our congregation of Jewish believers in *Yeshua* took place. These are, therefore, God's words spoken through Rabbi Martin Chernoff:

You are called to live in the resurrection life! You have been called to follow Yeshua into victory in your lives. You shall not say that you are defeated. You shall speak forth the Word of God. God watches you with eyes of compassion and love, day and night. God wants you to be delivered, as Peter was delivered even though Satan sought to sift him.

Look to the Lord your God, and realize that, as these days of sifting are upon you with God's permission, the days in which calamities will come upon this world, days in which the earth itself shall be reeling to and fro and even the elements of nature may break forth, God has given Satan permission in order to sift His people, in order to make His people strong in the Lord and in the power of His might.

You shall not say, "I cannot stand it," for God is allowing this, and you shall be protected. Those of you who truly trust in the Lord, who truly search your hearts and yield yourselves to God, and are looking for the power of God to fall, you shall be protected from the elements of nature and from Satanic attacks.

Do not worry about it, but pray and cast your burden upon the Lord, and He will sustain you. You shall say, "But why is this happening? We are so content here in America. "Because your God has better things for you. Because God wants to bring you into the revival that you are talking about, that you say you are praying about. God wants to answer your prayers.

He does have to shake the ones that call themselves the children of God, the ones who call themselves born of God's Spirit, for His children are complacent. And yet, many of them are being roused up already by the Spirit of God. They are but a small portion of His people. God has many people in this land who are still sleeping spiritually, who are not wide awake, or they do want to get wide awake, but they are allowing the things of the world to interfere. So God must move throughout this land and sift His people in order to wake them up spiritually, in order that they might be revived.

Revival does not come through earthly calamities. It comes by the Spirit of the living God. But in order to get His people to pray, in order to get His people to

A Prophecy by Rabbi Martin Chernoff

praise God even in the night seasons, He must sift this land because His people are not waking up.

For thirty years, He has sought in this land to wake up His people. Very few have awakened spiritually, but now He cannot wait any longer. The time is upon you. You must pray. You must call upon God. You must take time to fast and pray. You must wait upon God in the night seasons as well.

God says unto His people that He loves all of you. Thank God for the people who are serving God and following Him. He loves you in a special way because you belong to Him. God wants to bless you, but He cannot bless you until you are in a place of blessing. You must come forth now, for God cannot wait any longer, for prophecy is being fulfilled. The clouds and storms of prophecy are coming. The calamities of this world are going to come across this land and the whole world.

God is waiting to give us revival. He is going to shake us now. He has shaken us because He has waited thirty years, and now He cannot wait. He must move in answer to prayer.

God did not want to send calamity, but now He must in order to wake up His people. Even though He is reluctant to do it, He must move. And the power of God must fall because the time is short. Unless God begins to move, you will find greater calamities coming upon this country.

God is calling His people to prayer and intercession. God is calling you to wait upon Him and praise Him for the tremendous victories He has for you.

People of God, forget your differences and band together before it is too late for this country. Get together. Wake up, and God shall pour out His Spirit on all flesh.

And now, take spiritual stock of yourselves to see if you are in the faith. Take spiritual inventory and the God of blessing shall come upon you. You will find that God is ready to move. The Son is ready to move. The Spirit is ready to move. All of Heaven is ready to move. And now, you shall move as well. The power of God shall fall.

But, do not fear the calamities, for you shall be protected. You shall be protected if you are truly living for the Lord. You shall be protected. You shall come into the stronghold. The name of the Lord is a strong tower and the righteous enter into it and are saved.

Amen!

BIBLIOGRAPHY

American Hebrew-Christian, Vol.58:3, 1973, pp 13-14.

Ausubel, Nathan. *Pictoral History of the Jewish People.* New York: Crown Publ, 1953.

Birmingham, Stephen. *The Rest of Us.* New York, Berkley Books.

Baron, Salo. *The Russian Jew Under Tsars and Soviets.* New York: MacMillan, 1964.

_____. *The Jews in the Modern World.*

Chernoff, David. *Yeshua, the Messiah.* Havertown, PA: MMI P. 1983.

Epstein, Helen. *Children of the Holocaust.* New York: G.P. Putnam's Sons, 1979.

Fruchtenbaum, Arnold. *Hebrew Christianity: Its Theology, History & Philosophy.* Texas: Ariel Ministries, 1983.

Harrelson Walter, & Randall M. Falk. *Jews & Christians: A Troubled Family.* Nashville: Abingdon, 1990.

Hakiza, Ammi. *Ha-Karmel 7, No.1. D.* Goldman, trans. 1866.

Kac, Arthur W. *Messianic Hope.* Grand Rapids: Baker BH, 1990.

Liberman, Paul. *The Fig Tree Blossoms: Messianic Judiasm Emerges.* Harrison, AR: Fountain P, 1976.

Lindsey, Robert L. *Jesus, Rabbi & Lord.* Cornerstone, 1989.

Menkus, Belden. *Meet the American Jew.* Nashville: Broadman, 1963.

Portnov, Anna. *Awakening.* Baltimore: Lederer Press, 1992.

Rausch, David. *Messianic Judaism.* NY: Edwin Mellen Press, 1982.

Rodriguez, Victor.

Rubenstein, Amnon. *The Zionist Dream Revisited.* NY

Schocken Books, 1984.

Schaeffer, Edith. *Christianity Is Jewish.* Carol Stream: Tyndale House Press, 1977.

Schlink, Basilea. *Israel, My Chosen People,* trans. Old Tappen, NJ: Chosen, 1987.

Shamir, Ilana & Schlomo Shavit, eds. *Encyclopedia of Jewish History.* New York: Facts on File P, 1986.

Sorko-Ram, Shira. *I Became As A Jew.* Dallas: Maoz, 1991.

Stern, David H. *Messianic Jewish Manifesto.* Clarksville, MD: Jewish New Testament Press, 1991.

Uris, Leon. *Exodus.* New York: Doubleday, 1958.

Van Groningen. *Messianic Revelation in the Old Testament.* Grand Rapids: Baker BH, 1992.

Weber, Timothy P. *Living In the Shadow of the Second Coming.* Chicago: University of Chicago Press, 1987.

Winer, Robert I. The Calling: *The History of the Messianic Jewish Alliance of America, 1915-1990.* Wynnewood, PA: MJAA, 1990.

World Book Encyclopedia, Vol. 18 (6:9).

Yassen, Leonard C. *The Jesus Connection.* NY: Crossroad, 1986.

ARTICLES:

____. "President's Message." THE AMERICAN HEBREW CHRISTIAN, Vol. 57:1(1972):16-17.

____. "A Message from the President." THE AMERICAN HEBREW CHRISTIAN, Vol. 58:3 (1973):12-14.

Frydland, Rachmiel. "Great Events at Messiah '75." THE AMERICAN MESSIANIC JEWISH QUARTERLY, Vol. 60:3 (1975): 3-4.

Goldberg, Louis. "The Messianic Jew." *Christianity Today* 17 (February 1974): 494-499.

Golden, Harry. "Introduction." EXODUS by Leon Uris.

Henry, Carl F.H. "Jews Find the Messiah." *Christianity*

Bibliography

Today 18 (13 April 1973): 728-729.

Herzl, Theodor. "Judenstadt." 1896.

Juster, Daniel C. with Daniel W. Pawley. "A Messianic Jew Pleads His Case." *Christianity Today* 25 (24 April 1981): 587-589.

Plowman, Edward E. "Turning on to Jeshua." *Christianity Today* 16 (17 December 1971): 289-290.

Rausch, David. "The Emergence of Messianic Judaism in Recent American History." *Christian Scholars Review* 12 (1983): 157-166.

____. "Hebrew Christian Renaissance and Early Conflict with Messianic Judaism." *Fides et Historia* 15 (Spring/Summer 1983): 67-69.

____. "The Messianic Jewish Congregational Movement."

The Christian Century 99 (15 September 1982): 926-929.

Rich, Lawrence J. "A Look at the Origins and Development of the MJAA." *The American Messianic Jewish Quarterly, Vol. 64:5* (1979): 4-7.

Rosen, Martin Meyer. "Why are Young Jews Turning to Christ?" *Christianity Today* 17 (10 November 1972): 124-145.

Rosen, Moishe. "Plea for Unity." *The American Messianic Jewish Quarterly, Vol. 61:2* (1976): 17-18.

Made in the USA
Las Vegas, NV
16 July 2021